RESOLUTION

by Julian Palmer

Resolution by Julian Palmer

Copyright © 2025 by Julian Palmer

All rights reserved.

Published by Anastomose

Cover Art by Lachlan Wardlaw

https://othersideart.com.au

Cover design by Maryna Arsenieva

ISBN: 978-0-9925528-2-4

Dewey Number: 303.49

First Edition

Printed by Ingram Spark

http://www.julianpalmerism.com

CONTENTS

Chapter 1
Stupidity, Tyranny And Overpopulation............................ 09

Chapter 2
Let's Start Again.. 18

Chapter 3
Could We Go On? 25

Chapter 4
How Do We Do It? 34

Chapter 5
How We Could Be 47

Chapter 6
An Optimal Society For All Human Beings........................ 63

Chapter 7
We Should All Just Get Along 76

Chapter 8
Systems For Life 86

Chapter 9
How To Live 97

ACKNOWLEDGEMENTS

Resolution took an immensely long time to write, shape, and edit over nine years.

Many thanks to my editors and proofreaders over the years: Jennifer McMahon, Sofie Elofsson, David Elmore, and especially Angus Donald.

INTRODUCTION

The messages in this book began rippling up within me at the beginning of 2001, until I finally started writing them down in 2010. The process wasn't like writing from stone tablets or simply being inspired. The words came more from an insistent place in my consciousness. I took down notes, and when transcribing these, I realized that I was essentially communicating the same thing, maybe even four or five times over—which eventually gives the present text a spirit of holographic, repetitive lyricism.

Even though during this time I took a lot of psychedelics and had many visions and insights, the words here didn't arise out of one vision or a series of visions, but more from a place of inner knowing that does not need to be shown visions. Yet I am sure there are many who have had visions regarding this kind of material, and I have spoken to various people regarding their visions, which do align with this communication.

What I became aware of during this time of inspiration was that human evolution wanted to press forward into a spiritual fulfillment as its primary directive, and the flowering of the human species was its predominant directive. I could see there was a transition into a new human being and a new language. I was shown there would be a mass awakening in consciousness, even though I had difficulty understanding how that could be possible in my lifetime. I also undertook an education in parasitic entities and how to clear them. I was shown the potential for new ways of being and understood, to some degree, how humanity was evolving to become a new species.

In terms of my relation to this material, perhaps I am just gutsy enough and largely immune to other people's negative sentiments that this message could come through me. I shared some of these ideas with friends and on social media, and it became very clear to me that a lot of people wanted to hold onto the status quo, no matter how clearly uncomfortable or unworkable it is. Yet there were some other people I talked to who had similar opinions to mine.

Often, when I introduced these ideas to people, I was either ignored or received quite a lot of resistance. People would say things like, "Would you put your hand up first to be taken out by the aliens?" The answer is, "Yes, I would." I've already made that decision. There have been times in my life when I was not convinced I actually had the right stuff in order to live in a new kind of civilization.

Perhaps there could be a way humanity could trundle on with ten billion people, with all the challenges we face. Yet the gross inequality is so jarring, and ethno-nationalistic tribalism and religion appear much like a prison of suffering that few are willing to escape from. But most of all, people are not happy because we're increasingly looking at a dystopian society full of deception, brainwashing, and technocratic manipulation.

It clearly appears to me that the ecosystem of Earth is not meant to handle this many human beings, especially when you travel in highly populated countries like Indonesia, the Philippines, and India, as I commonly do, exploring the ecosystems of these countries while searching for psychoactive plants in the wild. Any more than a billion people on Earth looks like humanity in plague proportions, severely compromising all other animals and living systems, which is what we are seeing now, leading to a breakdown of environmental systems.

In every country I go to, the story is the same—the rich exploit the poor. IF the rich could work to the benefit of the poor, or even humanity in general, there could be massive shifts. But we are dealing with all sorts of IFs, with no clear sign any of these factors is ever going to change. How long could the human species and its descendants live in some type of sustainable civilization? A thousand years? A hundred thousand years? Millions of years? If humanity doesn't get this right this time, surely there will be an opportunity to "try again" at another time far into the future... but maybe not as well.

In the scale of these large time frames, each of our lives is not that important. I think it is important to keep in mind that each of us will die and leave behind all that we love on Earth one day. What makes us think our lives at this time on planet Earth are all that important? If we are to look at the human species as a whole, I think it makes sense to keep the parts of the planetary body of humanity that are somewhat healthy and workable, and let go of those parts that are unhealthy and toxic.

I'm not personally living in a religious state of mind, waiting for Judgment Day or the aliens to come and kill almost all of us. I live my life thinking how I can improve and make better what we have now, not really giving concern to any future "deliverance" or "rapture." I don't think waiting for such an event is a healthy idea, given that this is what religious people have been doing for millennia. I do think that within the next few decades humanity is reaching its global crunch point, and so it is not surprising that the long-anticipated "apocalypse" is likely to occur within this time frame.

I have recently been thinking about how we can reorganize political life and create systems in order to live in a more harmonious and collective manner. It is obvious to me that we need to get to work to create the most ideal systems and ways of life with what we have now. Much of humanity seems resigned or stuck, caught up in secondhand, inferior ways of living based on the dynamics of human power, which do not give priority to human dignity and the desire for people to have a real life.

I always had the feeling there was a right timing for the release of this book. I started to get truly serious about editing it during the COVID-19 crisis, which I feel has radically shifted humanity's understanding and which I hope will highlight many of the themes of this book. What some of us could clearly see is that humanity began to bifurcate into the minority who thought things through and the majority who just didn't really think at all.

I have faith that Earth will be cleared of this parasitic infection and that humanity will emerge from this collective insanity, however it occurs. That thought is so inspiring; no other thought or idea regarding the direction of humanity makes as much sense. Ultimately, this book was written to share this inspiration of what life could be, if indeed humanity is to be truly free.

Julian Palmer : September 2025

CHAPTER 1: STUPIDITY, TYRANNY AND OVERPOPULATION

This is how it begins

Stupidity is so ever-present in our global society, and the sad thing is that there is no solution for it. We are all banging our heads against a brick wall regarding an issue that cannot be solved. It is not the fault of the stupid people that they are stupid. They are a result of society itself, their own genetics, and their environment. Yet being stupid for them is a continual punishment, and our society punishes stupidity continually. Seeing as we cannot solve this issue in them or somehow heal it, the only answer to remove this suffering is to relinquish all the stupid people from Earth.

A true cleanup of the genetics of the human species is necessary if we are going to have any chance to survive as a species and thrive into the future. There is no way we can create a sustainable star farming civilization and bring along all of these unthinking people. What we are seeing very clearly now is that almost all of the functions of human beings in our society, in terms of work, can be replaced by AI, robots, and our technologies in ten years or less. How are we supposed to run a society when almost none of us are actually needed?

How many of us could differentiate ourselves from the AI and say we truly have something to give to society? All we have left as human beings is our presence, our love, our emotions, and our ability to connect. Therefore, a truly human society must be based upon these truly human qualities as a foundation, not least because these are the qualities that bring the most meaning to our lives.

Yet the real issue in humanity is deeper than the extant stupidity of the unthinking 99 percent. Humanity is enslaved by a tyranny that is not the bankers, the Jews, the billionaires, or the shadow world government, because it is invisible. If this tyranny were visible, we would have chopped off its head by now. The libertarian premises of Western civilization themselves are based upon revolution—for example, the French and American revolutions, which represent the overthrowing of tyranny. You can cut off the head of "the dominator culture," but unless you cut off the head of the etheric interference in the etheric, then it will simply express itself through other power structures within human society.

Within our society, to begin talking about an invisible etheric tyranny is often considered the height of insanity, as the tyranny itself inoculates you against believing in its existence, and culture typically punishes those who talk about this subject. Yet many people these days are waking up to these etheric entities that influence our society. What we can see is that these forces often control those with the most power in human society. As the saying goes, "Power corrupts, and absolute power corrupts absolutely." But this somewhat glib statement doesn't explain very much. What is clear is that this corruption is largely undetected or misunderstood by many people. We can observe that many of the people "at the top" clearly do appear to be evil or become evil. Grandfather conspiracy theorist David Icke believes that, at the very top, there are people around a table taking instructions from malevolent forces, and with all that is presently occurring in the world, more and more people could actually find this plausible.

The convergence between the occult and the elite of this world is not a mystery and can be observed in Masonic rituals, for example. In some sense, the people who believe they are the best of us very often become captured and co-opted to fulfill the agenda of malevolent forces. We can all wonder why it is that the rich seem not to truly do anything to transform our world in a positive way, something we ourselves could easily do. Sure, philanthropy is a thing, but too often this money appears to end up maintaining the status quo or just filling the hole, rather than making any real change that would truly better human society.

The average person on the street may appear confused and wonder what the shape and form of these malevolent beings could be. Many people in modern society have given up on the absurdity of religion and have chosen a more absurd "atheism," which ideologically doesn't give much space to the unseen or the unknown. When we speak of the etheric, we refer to an entirely different plane of existence, one that shamans throughout the ages have engaged with, communicating with the beings that inhabit it. Indeed, shamanism is defined by the dictionary as the communication and relationship with good and evil spirits.

Many people are waking up to this etheric dimension through the use of psychedelic tryptamines, which give us an access point into the mysterious and wondrous nature of these dimensions of existence. Tryptamines such as DMT allow access to these realms of consciousness and to the entities and beings within them, although it is not accurate to call these "DMT realms," as they are simply previously unseen planes of existence.

But there are horrifying realms and evils that we can encounter too. These perceptions accord with the basic precepts of almost all traditional cultures, and so it should not be surprising that human observations across those societies are correct as to the existence of "bad spirits." Western viewpoints often do a good job of bypassing or dismissing these "extrasensory" aspects of the human experience. If it cannot be measured, experience itself is somehow downgraded and disparaged as being merely "subjective."

Enlightenment-era perspectives would rather bypass the existence of evil as some sort of lack of good, or as ignorance, but clearly there is something else going on. When it comes down to it, many of these etheric beings are simply feeding upon human energy. When one becomes aware, it becomes clear that common feelings of being drained, having intrusive thoughts, being anxious, and having headaches are often symptoms of being fed upon by these beings.

We live in an anxiety epidemic and an epidemic of mental illness, but what is, in fact, mental illness in most cases, is actually interference and attachments from these entities. Many of them do exist or live within the human body, but it is more likely they will come at random times—especially around 3 a.m.—when the human protective shielding is at its weakest.

We can clearly see how the people around us disguise the madness and uncontrolled thinking they have. Human beings are rather good at hiding or obscuring their confused thoughts and emotions. This soup of madness, projection, and emotion represents the state of the typical person in our time. It is no wonder that modern people have such difficulty maintaining personal relationships in the mashed up confusions, contradictions, and inconsistencies of their own minds. It does take some effort to free oneself from these influences and to free one's mind so that the mind is not confused and out of control in its incessant thinking. Yet not everyone is strong enough to be free, and neither does everyone want to be free.

Our global civilization is being farmed and fed upon by these entities[1], and such entities believe they own us, similar to how farmers believe they own their animals. Different

---

[1] For a thorough exposition on this subject, please see my article "A Primer on Malefic beings."

https://julianpalmerism.com/primer-malefic-entities/

societies have different ways to manage life under such tyranny. In northern European societies, the collective effort appears to cut out emotionality, so that they are not, in fact, feeding the tyranny with too much somatic food. The issue with this approach is that it doesn't entirely work, as cutting out emotionality is not possible. However, you can see quite clearly how "the elite" in these northern European countries are perhaps the most unemotional people on Earth. As an overall tactic, this is not such a bad one. However, you are left with people unable to enjoy or experience a particularly rich life, as their wings are clipped and they live within narrow parameters set for them by their culture or community.

Some Asian cultures might align with certain entities, typically dragons, who then operate as guardians and protectors. This is no secret to anyone who has seen the dragons parading through the streets on Chinese New Year, or if you have been to a Chinese temple where depictions of the dragon predominate. These etheric dragons aim to take their piece of the human pie, as it were, and offer a kind of protection against other interference. This tactic is not a bad one, but such societies can still be steered in the direction of control, repression, and malevolence, and not according to the direction of people's highest aspirations.

Paganistic cultures align themselves with a grouping of "gods" who protect and serve them. In that sense, such cultures operate like a cult. In exchange for protection, the culture is continually offering the gods gifts and energy in various forms. The pictures on Egyptian temples, for example, are almost ninety percent depicting human beings offering gifts to the gods.

Other cultures may tend toward sacrificing animals, which makes no sense at all from a Western perspective. However, from their perspective, what they are doing is feeding the entities with an animal's energies, which then diverts the entities away from attempting to take human energy.

The tyranny that we all experience is a repression of the human spirit and represents a cultural control over what we say, how we say it, and what we don't say. Tyranny in most cultures is the rule, not the exception. The Western world is an anomaly in history, as we are experiencing a relatively untyrannical culture, and yet the tyranny remains, bubbling up to the surface, influencing and affecting all of us.

The quality people problem

With the overpopulation issue comes the dilution of useful, thoughtful, and conscious people, drowned out by unthoughtful and mechanistic individuals. Large numbers of mechanical people in a populace also create alienation, which is when there is little care given toward fellow human beings. People then become interchangeable and dispensable, so a caring social fabric becomes difficult to maintain. People cease to see much value in human fellowship when the quality of attention and the values offered by most people become denuded. Without much loyalty or significant value exchanges within the interpersonal realm, what foundation is there to build reliable and healthy relationships? Alienation and loneliness are perhaps the primary diseases of our time—and a much bigger issue, in terms of our individual and collective well-being, than many people realize.

Increasingly, it seems, people breed based on quite random biological and psychological desires. Class represents the idea that the most worthy are those descended from people who have accumulated the most wealth. Yet this is the most politically incorrect idea that conservatives do not quite clearly state. The opposite inclination of Pol Pot and the Bolsheviks is not eliminating the ruling class, but killing the poor and working classes, which is as brutal an idea as the most fatal and tragic conclusion of the communist class war. Clearly, both the presumably down to earth, warm, working class people and the assumed sophisticated, astute, well read aristocrat can display admirable qualities, as can the middle class secondary schoolteacher. However, if we think back to our days at school, most of our teachers were probably pretty average, if not awful. Maybe we had a handful of excellent teachers if we were very lucky, or most likely one or two who gave us some sense that there was sanity in the world.

Good people are to be found within every class or stratum, and it is difficult to assume that any social class is innately better than any other. The upper classes are much maligned in many leftist, post Marxist perspectives. The nobility has always justified its existence by claiming a higher kind of virtue or innate nobility, but surely such qualities are not homogeneously spread throughout the presumed upper classes. Increasingly, it seems, those who accumulate money are quite craven and insecure individuals appeased by status symbols and the things money can buy. It is most accurate to say that people of all strata demonstrate truly worthy human faculties, such as caring about others or having some natural talent in any given field. The idea that any particular social class is bringing humanity down is grossly simplistic and generally leads to tragic consequences.

Civilizations such as ours have allowed a lot of unexceptional, uninspiring, and often very troublesome people to exist. In most cultures, such people have become the majority. Truly troublesome and unexceptional people are generally weeded out in different ways within tribal societies, where people are forced to live and work with one another closely. For example, during coming of age initiations, the outcome may be death, or there may be severe punishment for breaking tribal law, including ostracism, spearing, or even "hunting accidents."

Spaceship Earth needs a new crew

How can we deal with a population of ten billion people hitting the wall of collective global catastrophe? Ten billion people are facing unstable weather, crop failures, droughts, water depletion, and an unsustainable, essentially unstable financial system, all within a global human culture not truly motivated to care for or look after itself, only to continue growing like a cancer. Ecologically, humanity has taken over most of the suitable land on Earth for farming, so already much of the forest has been cleared, and what natural habitat is left is often threatened. Humanity has become a pest, taking so much from the Earth but rarely giving back.

There are too many of us. Humanity is like a rabid plague of hungry rabbits, consuming as much as they can, with a single tenet inscribed on their value stone: "economic growth." For economic growth to continue, the human population must continue to grow, or else economic growth will reverse and the whole artificial game will start to crumble back into the sand. What we are now seeing is that population growth is slowing in the wealthier countries, yet continues to rise in many poorer regions. That population reduction in wealthier nations may harm their economic health within the current system is a clear sign of the absolute insanity of our models of reality, as reducing population and the consumption of natural resources is clearly what we should be doing.

So how can the rabbits' appetites be curbed? What would that look like? At present, our whole system promotes as much consumption as possible. What would a mode of being that promoted the least possible consumption look like? Is anyone, except for a tiny percentage of people, even remotely interested in creating or living in such a way? So much of what we do pollutes our environment, with narrow-mindedness inherent in our agendas. Most of us are still stuck in "survival" mode—us versus nature. Very clearly, cooperation with nature is a more intelligent way, but most of us barely know what this means.

Is there any hope of ten billion people successfully continuing to live on the planet? Ten thousand years of history have shown us that big civilizations eventually run out of resources, overextend through warfare, or see their crops fail due to exhaustion of the soil[2]. If we cannot change into a sustainable mode of existence, and if most are still blinded and blinkered by selfish greed and survival, what real hope is there? Perhaps there would not be a problem if our planet consisted of seven to ten billion intelligent people of conscience who respected the Earth and each other—individuals not just driven by greed and survival. But this is far from the case, as most people only care about themselves and maybe the lives of those closest to them.

We could all manage to live on spaceship Earth if we cared for one another and used our resources sustainably. As it stands, this care appears largely absent—except in the wealthiest countries, where some can actually afford to care. What could stop our systematized overconsumption other than complete catastrophe? And catastrophe is guaranteed if we continue to do what we are doing. This insanity is not working for most of us. What we are doing now is the very definition of madness. How can this madness be stopped, and another way introduced, except by a complete interruption? What is clear is that this insanity will not stop of its own accord. It will need to be deliberately stopped. Humanity requires an absolute reset.

---

[2] "In the last 40 years, humans have destroyed a third of Earth's farmland. Soil is now blowing or washing away 100 times faster than it can form, and without that soil, humans may not be able to feed their growing population, according to an analysis of research published over the past decade. To avert disaster, say researchers, governments need to help farmers adopt sustainable agricultural practice." https://www.theguardian.com/environment/2015/dec/02/arable-land-soil-food-security-shortage

CHAPTER 2: LET'S START AGAIN

No more superfluousness

Can anyone say with a straight face that human life, hurtling onward, propelled by consumerism, is at all sustainable or viable for another 50, 100, or 200 years? At what point does a global civilization cease to circle the marketplace and change direction toward truly human values? And more importantly, HOW does a civilization move away from being one where most people are just surviving to one where everyone is thriving?

Again, it does appear humanity is at plague proportions, and with the sheer number of people on the planet, there is a dilution of admirable human qualities. Our genetics are not strong as a species, appearing to be weakened and watered down by a culture in which the whims and desires of the unthinking predominate. As the 19th century German philosopher Friedrich Nietzsche stated, "All too many are born,"[3] and he said that about "the superfluous ones" when the world population was perhaps only 1.5 billion people.

Sometimes it would appear that there only need be a certain number of talented individuals in any given landmass—just a few stars in the human drama, and many extras. Perhaps the Earth itself is a computer, some sort of motherboard with only a limited amount of RAM and human

---

[3] The full quote is from Nietzsche's philosophical diatribe *Thus Spake Zarathustra* and reads "all too many are born: for the superfluous the State was invented." The section of the book from which the quote is extracted is largely an exposition on what Nietzsche calls the "superfluous ones." Much could be written about Nietzsche's interpretation, yet he considers them to be an inherently unnecessary people, committed to regurgitation and foolishness, who also constitute the predominant people in society. The superfluous ones are counterpointed with Nietzsche's view of the Übermensch, often wrongly termed "superman," yet it is perhaps more accurate to understand Nietzsche's Übermensch to represent a man who evolves through forging his own unique path in life, full of meaning and purpose.

processes it needs to fulfill, as the Non Player Character (NPC) meme creator asserted.[4]

Humanity as a whole is evolving to a new state, an interconnected existence, where our innate spiritual nature can flower and come to the fore. Many visionaries over the last hundred years have prophesied a new way of being and, consequently, a new world for humanity as an evolutionary potential.[5] In this evolution, many individuals are going to get left behind simply because they cannot express the higher-order functioning of this inner human technology, as that capacity is simply not present in them. It appears that the seeds of a higher evolution exist within the very few, and not within the majority. For evolution to proceed, it seems that it is only necessary that the few prevail in order to let those seeds within them develop to fruition.

For the majority of souls who are not able to engage with, enter, or function in the new world, we must ask: "Where would they go?" Presumably, they must go somewhere, wherever that might be. If you do not believe in life after death, then their death is simply the end of them. If you believe that we are all absorbed back into universal consciousness after death, then that is where they would end up. If you believe they continue their evolutionary journey as souls, then perhaps each of them will go to different places within the

---

[4] https://en.wikipedia.org/wiki/NPC_(meme)
An anonymous post on 4chan catalyzed the popular Non Player Character (NPC) meme, which has entered everyday language very quickly: "I have a theory that there are only a fixed quantity of souls on planet Earth that cycle continuously through reincarnation. However, since the human growth rate is so severe, the soulless extra walking flesh piles around us are NPCs, or ultimate normalfags, who autonomously follow group think and social trends in order to appear convincingly human." The popularity and resonance of the NPC meme go to show that a lot of people agree that there are many people on Earth who believe that overpopulation has created a whole new breed of people, (the majority) who are not actually autonomous in their thinking. Although these perceptions are funny, they are also tragic. You could say the meme has transcended being a temporary trend, and the word has now become a part of regular parlance. New Age writer Dolores Cannon also presents the concept of "backdrop people" in her book The Convoluted Universe: Book 4—those people who are extras on the movie set of Earth, who don't truly have a soul, and who are not actively engaged in personal growth or spiritual evolution but instead serve as placeholders in the backdrop of reality

[5] Visionaries such as Teilhard de Chardin, Sri Aurobindo, Jean Houston, Barbara Marx Hubbard, Rudolf Steiner, and Emanuel Swedenborg.

greater cosmos to continue their journey. Can we humans ever know for sure what happens after death for each human being?

It has often been said that if every species could vote, do you think they might vote humanity on or off the planet? And what if every animal on Earth could vote to reduce the population of humanity to fifty million people, with those remaining humans becoming responsible citizens who wouldn't pollute or create war? Do you think they might decide to actually keep us humans, if not actually welcome our presence on Earth?

Suppose that only the most capable people remained, and then those people went on to breed with one another. In this case, the most desirable genetic factors within the species would be perpetuated. The resulting all—around capable people would then create a conducive environment—a new culture that enriches and supports human beings rather than corrupting and dragging them down through mechanistic and commercial imperatives. Then both primary factors recognized as enabling humans to be what they are—genetics and environment—would be optimized. We would be leaving the very best humans to create a world that fundamentally works—a world in harmony with nature, in which all human beings are actually enjoying themselves and their lives. Issues such as warfare, poverty, and alienation would be eradicated as vestiges of a dysfunctional and immature species.

Utopia is the only direction in which to go

Some sort of "perfect" utopian world is a kind of fantasy, at least in the near future. Perhaps there is too much immaturity, confusion, dysfunction, and trauma to clear within the epigenetics of the species before we can come to a collective equanimity and truly get along together—surely a huge collective work, if ever there was one.

However, we could live in a world that supports our human growth instead of encouraging us to act like imbecilic children enslaved to the almighty dollar. First and foremost, we need to create an ecologically sustainable civilization as a foundation for life and then build upon that foundation to create an equitable collective human lifestyle. Upon that foundation, we can collectively work toward balance and alignment, coming to a true connection within ourselves and with the natural world.

Given the chance, human beings know how to create rich, fulfilling lives by reaching out to one another and facilitating genuine interpersonal connections and collective action. With stimulus and guidance from elders, the empowerment of the youth, and due respect given to the creative and the wise, it would not be too hard for all of us to create a meaningful collective and individual lifestyle for every human being.

The end of capitalism

The system of consumer capitalism is simply an extension of the basic buying and selling of the "medieval" marketplace, and in no way represents a culture that is intelligent, self-organizing, or humane—a culture in which people can truly live and express who they are.

The primary problem with the global capitalistic system is that almost all of us are still ensnared within the realm of survival, although there is nothing wrong with pursuing survival per se. Surviving is an endeavor that motivates most people to get out of bed in the morning and do their duties to themselves, their families, and their society. But we must evolve and grow beyond survival and choose to live in ways that are not forced, that arise from our individual and collective will, so that our actions are intrinsically rewarding and motivated, and we each have a desire to build a useful life within a society based upon meaningful and rewarding activity.

More than half the world's population lives in poverty and is forced to focus primarily on just surviving. If you are one of the hundreds of millions of people in the world who are hungry and all you can think about is where to get enough food to eat, then it is going to be hard to live when the little you can get may not give you enough sustenance for a healthy mind and body. It is difficult to live when all day you are working in a factory carrying out repetitive motions, and you are only getting enough money to survive, and maybe just enough to provide for your family. This is not humane. Many such factory workers may even be worse off than prisoners in Western jails. As a team, humanity is letting itself down by allowing these conditions to prevail. How can we say we live in anything like a civilized world when so many of us are effectively enslaved in such terrible conditions?

Only human beings can care. Governments cannot care, and corporations certainly cannot care. Most corporations and governments typically represent sociopathic agendas that push individuals to act in ways not aligned with an internal ethic or common sense. Governments and corporations represent conservatively compromised politics that have lost sight of what is important, valuable, and even necessary for human beings. Lack of caring is a disease caused by a lack of contact and empathy with a primary human reality. Indeed, caring means to be connected to what is present. In our increasingly depersonalized and technocratic society, human beings so often become calloused and jaded by their fellow human beings and their petty agendas, and many people lose the ability to care.

Governed by the wise, not a system

Socialism is just a version of the marketplace, whereby the marketplace itself comes under central control—"control" being the key word here. There are no forms of socialism or communism that propose any true human values or ideal modes of existence beyond the means of production or modes of survival. All forms of socialism or communism known in our world have mostly been totalitarian ventures—tyrannical systems that enslave the people into limited belief systems and actions, often crippling or stifling the individual and limiting human freedom to a high degree. The failures of tyrannical forms of communism do not mean that any collective form of human existence which honors the individual and creates space for humans to "do their own thing" and remain independent and free is not possible or desirable. It is only our limited imagination and the existence of deeper tyrannical forces that prevent a truly individual and free, collective and connected, creative and caring society.

Human society should clearly be governed and directed by the intelligent, the thoughtful, the empathic, and the wise—not by economic imperatives, corporations, or the investor class. The marketplace cannot or should not govern human beings and their behavior. The marketplace cannot provide any guidance or intelligent feedback related to our humanity, yet this is the default world most of us live in. The marketplace only provides goods and services, and within the system, most of the spaces of our human existence occur in the framework of providing those goods and services—a nonsensical way of creating space for our individual and communal life force. Furthermore, the marketplace, in all its forms, is our most convenient baseline or common space, but the proffered goods and services in the marketplace stand between us, buffering and inhibiting our interpersonal possibilities.

Neither should human beings be governed by those who seek power or are controlled exclusively by a class of those who have accumulated the most money and power. The idea of noblesse oblige[6] is one in which the aristocracy once felt some obligation to look after their peasants, and this idea has almost been completely disregarded in our time. Now we largely have pragmatic businesspeople or corporations who treat people in an expendable manner. It does not even need to be said or explained that corporations are innately sociopathic and do not care about mere "people," as many of us face the inhumanity of "the system" on a daily basis.

---

[6] Noblesse oblige is a term that describes how the nobility must act in a responsible and generous manner with social responsibilities to those lower in rank, in a manner according to the height of their station in society.

CHAPTER 3: COULD WE GO ON?

We deserve more

Civilization could fumble on and go through cycles of dystopia, dysfunctional degradation, and the inequitable crushing system with all its entropy and technology. Some justify the status quo and say this is what humanity wants, what humanity deserves, as this framework has all the elements that humans need to learn their lessons, or that this is the inevitability of what our collective decisions must lead to. However, it is probably most useful to see the collective human body as one that is sick and out of alignment. If we are able to heal the collective human being, then individual human beings can work through what they need to in order to learn and grow and step forward evolutionarily.

This civilization is clearly intractable. There are inherent obstacles that lie within all the egotism, greed, stupidity, and tribalism that bring humanity down. Self-hatred lies at the heart of so many, because they don't even meet their own expectations of themselves. This society doesn't make good people. Many people love their pets more than they love themselves or others. Some people feel that this civilization is scheduled for demolition or decommissioning, which is an almost palpable sensation at times, affecting the mental health of everyone.

What we see in industrial civilization is the overdevelopment of the mental faculties, leading to a disconnect from emotional and empathetic values, from the body, from the Earth, and from each other—a kind of hyper-individuated alienation. We can also perceive in the individual human body a lot of stress in the musculature;

any massage therapist will tell you this is the norm. If you are a shiatsu or acupuncture practitioner, you will observe that persistent blockages in the meridian system are the norm. Any psychologist will tell you the depths of the mental and emotional issues of the people who come to see them. It is no news that severe mental and emotional imbalance in humanity is quite widespread. Why should it be any other way when our society has abnegated its humanity for the mercantile interests of a system that doesn't serve humanity and tends to work against most people?

However, we must consider that there could be a possibility of transitioning this society as it is, without taking any drastic measures. Any way you look at it, the result of just attempting to drag all these people into the future is more disparity, more inequality, and more suffering. Certainly, a small number of people could move away from the system and model a life together that co-regulates each other's nervous systems, and they could begin to actualize a more spiritual way of human life. Certainly, an ethical cult is possible, as long as malefic influences are going to be resisted. What if those people who are capable of living in this manner find a way to co-exist with industrial, corporate society? Surely, corporate society would find this to be offensive if small groups of people lived in a hypothetical paradisiacal harmony?

Even if you were to establish a small country and create a better system, we cannot expect the rest of the world to follow suit and adopt a more natural, equitable, and healthy way of life. It seems that only a small number of people would even be capable of living in anything like a utopian society, leaving the rest of society out in the cold, which is not really fair.

One of the primary issues we see in our society is a real lack of care for the less capable. There is something in us that sees fit to punish the less capable and call them words like "trailer trash." There are all kinds of names for the underclasses of the world, such as "untouchables," which makes the present inequality we do have quite inhumane.

There is a deeper issue that goes beyond how humans presently function, and that is the activation of new evolutionary forms of being. Only a small percentage of people will be able to engage with the new forms of human evolution, estimated at 0.5 to 1 percent of the present human population, and that's about 50 to 100 million people.

It is likely that, at some point, many of those from the "trailer trash" or "untouchable" class are suddenly activating new forms of beingness, while those from the merchant banker class are simply not cut out for any kind of connective sensitivity, so aligned are they with their own self-interest and imprisoned by tyranny. It might also well be that many people from the lowest rungs of society don't have enough intelligence or capacity for living in a new type of society.

A new society that might spring up from our own would naturally consist of a new type of natural aristocracy. Those who do not spiritually activate should naturally want to serve those who are already activated into these new forms of being. Yet people who are awakening to higher consciousness don't actually need or want a bunch of slaves to serve them, nor do they desire to lord over the masses and have power over them. This is a repugnant old paradigm that perpetuates inequity and grates on all of humanity. It is may be the case that perhaps a natural aristocracy will always exist within humanity, and the true natural aristocracy are those who desire most to serve others, give true value to their society, and reap the resulting rewards of doing so.

With the current evolutionary forces appearing to coincide with technological advancements, almost all of what we know is becoming redundant and unnecessary. Humanity clearly has a deep need to vanquish gross inequality completely—and the only way to do that is not to destroy the rich or bourgeoisie, as communism tended to do, nor to completely eradicate the poor, but to relinquish all those human beings who cannot meet the higher ethical and moral standards of a truly connected, humane, and sane society. Humanity needs a new ethos and a new operating system, and very few people can meet the higher standard. So, for the majority to live within a framework where they cannot truly experience that magic would be a kind of torture. Leaving them alive and only serving those who live in a spiritually actualized state would be a kind of unbearable fate for them.

It is humanity—all of us—that decides our own future. Humanity is, in fact, one being, an oversoul traditionally called 'God' that people who smoke 5-MeO-DMT are increasingly connecting with. This "God" is living through all of us and is sure to be sick and tired of the machinations of industrial society. We can only assume that God wants humanity in balance and alignment and not in plague proportions stacked on top of one another, struggling to just survive. Humanity (aka God) wants to live in peace, happiness, radiance, and beauty, fulfilling its dreaming. We must assume the destiny and desire of humanity is to live as tribal people traditionally have lived—in relative harmony, connection, and relationship, not in anxiety, depression, alienation, scarcity, and desperation.

Humanity doesn't want to live within the tired old religious and racial conflicts. Perhaps the only way to resolve them is via a complete reset that renders such disputes obsolete and leaves only the mentally sound people standing on Earth—those with no interest in perpetuating warfare and division or even continuing on with the ridiculous rituals of religion. Humanity wants to live in radiance and happiness, developing its ability to converse in universal languages and connect in authentic ways. It doesn't take much to perceive that our primary human function is to connect with each other and generate love. Those who have deep psychedelic experiences, mystical experiences, or near—death experiences commonly have this realization. Yet, this is also a great work, and we must give up being sold out to materialism and come back to our soul: its ability to connect, converse, and open up to spirit through each other.

The truth of what human beings are is souls expressed in human bodies. We are a bioelectric field[7] that no robot can replicate. We are an advanced technology already. The transhumanist folk often do not have the intellectual frameworks or the humility to understand this, because they may not be in contact enough with that potential within themselves. We need to become operational in a relational sense, in a sexual sense. We need to have orgasms—true orgasms—as Wilhelm Reich[8] defined them, essential for human emotional and psychic health. Humanity is presently gripped in a vice of social and religious repression of sexual and relational forces, trapped within a maze of mental and emotional tyrannies that prevent true prioritization and action.

Ultimately, we want to play, we want to have fun, we want to be in families and friendship groups, connected to nature and stimulated to grow and evolve. What everyone appears to want is this reality, yet it seems impossible for the majority of people to conceive of this potential actually occurring for them.

---

[7] The term bioelectric field refers to the expression of the body as a living field of energy, not just a physical body, but an expression of vital electromagnetic energy, called prana in the subcontinent, chi in China, and termed orgone by Wilhelm Reich.

[8] Wilhelm Reich, the Austrian psychoanalyst, writer, and inventor, defined the orgasm as an energetic discharge and release of energy, involving involuntary mutual contractions caused by the protoplasmic energetic—or orgone—connection between two human bodies. Reich saw most people as suffering from orgiastic impotence, meaning they were not able to connect in full emotional aliveness with their partner, causing emotional repression and dysregulation in society he called "the emotional plague."

Ideal conditions for life

Rather than thinking in terms of survival or how we are going to do the things we need to survive, we need to think about the ideal living conditions for human beings. Clearly, most of us know that living a life of so-called luxury or comfort is not the optimal way, and neither is living a spartan lifestyle. We know that nature, and connecting to nature and the natural world, is extremely good for human health, and that community and true human connection are perhaps the most important factors in well-being and happiness for human beings.

There is another factor: we cannot just expect that an ordinary life where "nothing much happens" is enough. On one hand, a life with too much stress will kill you, yet a life with no stress at all will leave you languid, without strength or resistance. Human beings who do not have any meaningful stressors in their lives do not become resilient and strong. Many people with high living standards in the West exist in a state where they effectively become weakened, without anything much to push back against in their coddled reality, leading to all kinds of pedantic weaknesses and dysfunctionality.

It would make sense, then, that if we do not naturally experience the factors that give us resilience and challenges in our "ultra-civilized" way of life, we must create them ourselves. The present reality we live in is, in some sense, a manufactured game, and it is manufactured in the sense that the forces that create difficulty and struggle are implicit within the system. However, there comes a time when humanity must grow up and transcend the need for artificial forms of struggle from a presumed other.

What we must do within the entire structure of our collective human sphere is create a place where optimal human learning occurs—neither too hard nor too easy, just like any good video game. The maze of bureaucratic and corporate complexities and limitations we find within the modern world, which constrain, constrict, and create barriers, offer more annoyance than real human challenge.

To be human is to know and be known within a framework of potential emotional expression. A tribal group of humans will engage with the natural world together to survive, and, in doing so, will navigate the complexities of interpersonal communication, which is challenging enough. Modern, alienated people stuck in the rat race generally do not have much in the way of meaningful human relational challenges. The framework of corporate life itself typically doesn't recognize your human needs in any way, shape, or form.

Yet even with a humanity that has its survival needs met, there still remains the need for love, and also the need for growth and self-actualization, which can only come from engaging with other humans. Once humanity realizes it is through the bioenergetic field that we empower one another, then we can conceive another kind of game, or way to be, one based on connection, rather than adversarial competition.

Freedom from the parasites is true health

As renowned spiritual teacher Alan Watts[9] has said, humanity wants to live in a spiritually fallen state, in a mediocre state, where it has forgotten who and what it is. From this perspective, humanity doesn't want to know what it is—it wants to forget. Perhaps what is often missing from these

---

[9] "Now when God plays hide and pretends that he is you and I, he does it so well that it takes him a long time to remember where and how he hid himself. But that's the whole fun of it — just what he wanted to do. He doesn't want to find himself too quickly, for that would spoil the game. That is why it is so difficult for you and me to find out that we are God in disguise, pretending not to be himself. But when the game has gone on long enough, all of us will wake up, stop pretending, and remember that we are all one single Self — the God who is all that there is and who lives for ever and ever."
From *The Book: On the Taboo Against Knowing Who You Are*, by Alan Watts.

viewpoints is the understanding that humanity is subject to a parasitic infection. What this means is that for whatever reason, there has been an incursion into the collective and individual psyche in most cultures. People are subject to "intrusive thoughts," a mentally unstable state of suffering whereby it is clear the aim is to bring humanity down, and that any attempts to lift humanity "up" are punished by these forces.

IF humanity is going to thrive, it must be sovereign, not infested or overly influenced by these etheric parasites. The issue is that most humans are effectively good producers of energy for these beings; they are farmed. You can do all you want to remove the parasites, but it is pointless if the people who remain on Earth continue to create food for more parasites to come in. That is why humanity must consist of those who are mentally strong enough to not continue to feed the parasites.

After the loss of the vast majority of the human population (who are creating the food for these entities), the remaining human beings would be able to effectively destroy the remaining etheric parasites and proceed to guard planet Earth to prevent more of these beings from engaging with us. Even more significantly, if humanity can then collectively live in a state in which very little negative emotion and errant thinking are being generated, then no food is being created to attract these beings in the first place. Free of these parasites, humanity would be much less inclined toward divisive and binary ways of thinking—the type of thinking that creates divisive belief systems, religions, and war in the first place.

Living on a planet free of these parasitic beings would feel—and be—completely different. Primarily, we would no longer be enslaved by irrationally mean parameters, nor have to live within psychic frameworks in which these beings severely constrain us. We would no longer be living on a farm where we are the farm animals, a system that does not work for us, but largely against us. We would feel a deep sense of safety and not have to brace ourselves against the irrationalities of how these entities express themselves through other people or through ourselves. As a whole, then, humanity could express more positive than negative emotions, and people could begin to experience more pleasure than suffering. Humanity could realize its true spiritual purpose and function.

Only once we eliminate these parasites from within the collective human body do we have a chance of living sanely and peacefully with one another. Clear of these entities between us, we can live in a more unified manner, thinking and acting in ways that are collectively beneficial for ourselves and for the Earth.

Torping[10] is the name I gave to a type of sound that effectively kills these parasites. It is a short, sharp sound, like a dog barking. There are also other methods people have developed to clear these entities, but torping is something most people can learn relatively easily. If everyone knew how to clear these entities and defend themselves from them, humanity would essentially be mentally healthy, with no forces to put human beings into mentally unbalanced states of being that cause suffering.

---

[10] For more detailed information about the technique torping and its utilization as a healing modality, see http://www.torping.com

CHAPTER 4: HOW DO WE DO IT?

Perspectives

Some people are so appalled by the state of the human species that they believe humans should be wiped out and the Earth completely given back to nature. The number of people who privately (and even publicly) think this way may be surprisingly large, and their numbers are likely growing. If, indeed, it were possible to wipe out all human beings, you would also have to wipe out the ecology of the Earth (such as in a large-scale nuclear catastrophe), and that would mean it might take hundreds or even thousands of years for ecological recovery to occur.

Many people feel hopeless and despairing in our present civilization, exasperated and demoralized by the lack of character and quality of people around them. They feel that eradicating all human beings is the only reasonable solution to what appears to be an existential quagmire. Perhaps there is another option which is viable, because decent and capable people still exist. Perhaps we could imagine a world that would consist only of sane, able, and truly humane people who actually care about humanity. Then human beings would stand a good chance of fulfilling an enriching evolutionary destiny.

However, what good would that option be for the great majority of humanity, who would face death if that course of action were taken? Wouldn't that be the ultimate slap in the face—that you are not "good enough" to live in the new world? How would you feel if you did not make the grade, and most of the people you know didn't make the grade either? If this were the ultimate sacrifice, then how many people would consciously choose it?

Throughout human history, countless millions of soldiers have made great sacrifices fighting for their king or country, commonly resulting in their death. But would the average person be prepared to give up their life for the sake of the biggest cause of all—the fate of the human species itself? Giving up one's life so the human species can hopefully live on Earth consciously and without war is an enormous sacrifice, with an outcome much greater than humanity has ever known.

Paradoxically, the people who would give up their lives for the sake of a conscious and sustainable human future are likely to be the very people who would be most suited to living in that future, and vice versa. The people most resistant to giving up their lives might well be the more selfish individuals who care for little else than their own. The length of a generation is ultimately so short in relation to the span of the evolutionary process of humanity—hundreds of thousands of years—that to lose the majority of human beings from any given generation is perhaps not such a big deal, at least from an impersonal and detached perspective.

There is no clear way forward as we are

The question I think many people contemplate is: What can we do now? Do we wait for Judgment Day? Do we wait for the complete destruction of our civilization—massive crop failures, global catastrophe caused by climate change, rising sea levels, global war, pandemics, financial disasters, and the emergence of AI?

More likely, we will see the steady decline of the global empire as we continue to flog the dead horse of our unsustainable system. As people increasingly escape into the screen—away from human interactions, relationships, or the "real world"—

collective mental health statistics go into free fall, and our technocratic civilization becomes literally sterile, miserable, and manipulated by tyrannical forces into a dystopian hell world of The Hunger Games.

Or could we bridge the gross inequities between millions of people in poor countries and the rich? Is it possible that billions of people could enjoy a comfortable, middle-class life—driving cars, flying on planes, eating beef, and using lots of fresh, clean water? Even if that were possible, would it be desirable? The answer appears clear: the purely consumeristic way of life is not worthwhile, considering the ever—increasing rates of drug addiction, anxiety, loneliness, relational breakdowns, and depression in most developed countries. The terrain of our society doesn't encourage or foster worthwhile people; it encourages brainwashed people—those who do what they are told, don't think for themselves, and have no commitment to any true values or ethics beyond their own selfish desires. We are an unhealthy society, full of mostly unhealthy people in mind and body, heading in the wrong collective direction. We are increasingly enslaved by systems that do not at all serve us as a species, lacking any true moral, ethical, or spiritual direction to guide us toward a sane, desirable way of life. A collective crash into the rocks is inevitable unless we can adjust course and begin to collectively proceed in the right direction.

Already we are seeing that the resources of our planet, such as fresh water, coal, and oil, are increasingly limited or compromised. Conceivably, humanity could act much more efficiently and limit our use of resources to a sustainable level. The real issue is that the whole system itself is designed to increase the use of resources, so it is difficult to see that limiting consumption would be possible without humans giving up the system itself and creating another. This seems highly unlikely. There are no indicators that such radical change is even being contemplated as an option by anyone other than a minority.

Many people are despondent because they can't see the viability of the available options. They believe Earth cannot support nine to ten billion people optimally. Climate science looks increasingly stark, with a seemingly inevitable warming of a few degrees causing a chain of catastrophic events for the human species, no matter whether you believe that warming is caused by human beings or not.

The Earth's biosphere clearly cannot sustain our level of unintelligence, systemic wastefulness, and overuse of resources. There is a good chance the system could collapse sooner rather than later. In fact, many people believe in this inevitable collapse, with the popular rise of prepper culture—those people who are preparing now for a life in a collapsed society. Assuming the "empire" collapses and we return to a relatively primitive way of life as foretold in many dystopian narratives, the physically strong and intelligent would survive, and perhaps the uncompromising rules of Mother Nature would come back to the fore.

If we are indeed doomed along our present trajectory, then we need to put all options on the table and consider some radically different trajectories. Overpopulation is the elephant swaying in the room, yet few want to admit (let alone address) this issue head-on. Yes, the developed countries are at times decreasing their populations, which is clearly going to cause all kinds of stressors on these societies, yet many developing nations are going to increase their populations dramatically, causing increased tensions in these parts of the world.

Are ten billion or even nine billion people going to live until 2100? There are many ominous predictions that make business as usual difficult for the human species. Any way you look at it, humanity likely has until about 2040 before these challenges prevent the current system from continuing. Even if we manage to survive as a global civilization by 2100, would we be able to bring half the population out of poverty? Would we, as a human society, be truly happy, let alone healthy in body and mind? Would we be heading in the right collective direction? Nobody knows for sure, but our civilization appears to be heading backward onto the ropes as tyrannical forces increasingly rear their heads. There are collective challenges that most of our systems appear unprepared or unwilling to deal with in any serious manner, as they themselves become corrupted, captured, and co-opted by the mind numbing tyranny.

Who gets to live is who can live

We need to consider the option that humanity may need to be "culled," as horrifying as this idea may appear. And if we don't cull ourselves, who or what is going to cull us? Could it be that a supernatural, heavenly force—known as God or Allah and His angels, as foretold in the Koran and the New Testament—does the job? Jesus talked of "God" pruning the vine that does not bear fruit[11]. Yet what is that fruit? As physical fruits do not appear from our human arms and hands, surely such a metaphorical fruit must be metaphysical in nature.

The apocalypse, as a natural event in which Gaia brushes humans off her body with cataclysmic events, would represent nature's cull. This might mean massive earthquakes, tsunamis, or huge asteroids and the like, or perhaps there might be a series of events of a longer, more subtle duration, in the form of infectious diseases, volcanic eruptions, crop failures, severe droughts, rising sea levels,

---

[11] Jesus's quote: "A healthy tree cannot bear bad fruit, nor can a diseased tree bear good fruit. Every tree that does not bear good fruit is cut down and thrown into the fire." Matthew 7:16-20

and unbearable temperatures.

Or, if Gaia doesn't cull us, could it be that a life form from another planet could perform such a cull? In that case, they would need a technology that could ascertain which humans are to survive and which humans would not. Perhaps such a cull could be carried out with the push of a button by such an advanced intelligence. I would suggest that we, as a species, would have to collectively agree to this cull—even proactively agree on the necessity of such an extraordinary action.

Assuming we, as a species, have asked a much more advanced species to push that button, we then don't know who gets to live and who doesn't. It's a lottery, and the odds are stacked against almost all of us. We could only hope that people of goodwill, initiative, intelligence, and cooperation are the ones who remain on our third rock from the Sun.

Or is there another possibility? Could we do the culling ourselves? If so, how would 90-99 percent of the population be persuaded to give up their lives, the most precious thing they have, so that a very few could live in a presumably much better world? If we really had to do the cull ourselves, how would it be possible to show people it was absolutely necessary? At this point, it is difficult to see a situation where such a cull would be agreed upon, except by a small, so-called elite who would want to force their will upon the greater populace when they no longer need the serfs to run society. The issue here is that these so-called elites are clearly not the diverse crew of spaceship Earth who can activate evolution and God's will for human life.

The most radical step

Perhaps the first step is to recognize that we, as a species, need to take this crucial step. The second step is to communicate to humanity and the cosmos that you believe in this outcome. As programmers of this reality, as co-creators in the truest sense of the word, we all have a say in the destiny of humanity. I believe that if we understand why this kind of intervention is most likely our best chance, then formal proceedings can begin with an advanced alien race. We also can't discount that many people are already in communication with different alien races, and there are many people worldwide practicing protocols such as CSETI[12], which are designed to contact alien races. It also seems likely that such alien races are already aware of us and will reach out when the time is right.

The intention of this book is to help set in motion these ideas, hoping there is a critical mass of intelligent and sensible people who agree this most radical step is the right way forward—IF indeed it truly is the right way forward. Presumably, there are advanced alien races who already know about our predicament. Just as we know about the overpopulation of animal species or the threat of extinction of different species, it makes sense that highly advanced alien races have the same level or duty of care to the cosmos that we have to Earth.

---

[12] The CSETI protocol, developed by Dr. Steven M. Greer, is a set of practices aimed at establishing peaceful contact with extraterrestrial intelligence. It involves group meditation, remote viewing, and visualization to create a coherent mental state, followed by signaling with lights, sounds, and coherent thoughts to attract and guide extraterrestrial craft. Participants document any phenomena observed and maintain clear, peaceful intentions throughout the process. The goal is to foster meaningful, nonthreatening communication with extraterrestrial beings.

Intelligent design?

It is a lot to comprehend—that in a large culling, most everyone would die: whole families, dynasties, corporations, the banking system, property, money. Almost everything we know in our world would have to come to an end. Then, and only then, in this total reset from utter death and destruction, could a new world be created—not from the ashes, but completely anew. Is there any other possible way this sort of complete reset could be executed except through such a culling?

Our species apparently needs an impartial authority without an overt agenda that must be aware of our primary problem and can help us solve it. But how would such an alien race determine the people who should live? Perhaps they could measure a good heart and perceive whether a person has intelligence, common sense, humanity, or the qualities of an overall sound human being. Perhaps there is a deeper signature in each human being, even in the genetic structure, which signifies an individual's suitability for life in a much more advanced society, which appears to be the more likely signal they would be looking for.

Could it be possible that after such a cull, the only people left on Earth might be Mormons, heavy metal kids, or Tahitians? I doubt it. It's highly unlikely that any one race or people who belong to certain belief systems would make it just because of their beliefs. Those cults, religions, or genetic groups that believe they are the chosen group only demonstrate their own tribal absurdity. How silly would it be to think that a certain group was the only one to be taken forward or desired in the next stage of human evolution? That is not to say that all Mormons, heavy metal kids, or Tahitians would not be wanted. But a world full of white-skinned American Christians wearing suits is a sick idea of heaven.

No, it is not homogeneity that is wanted—it is DIVERSITY. That diversity can then selectively interbreed, creating a stronger and more unique genetic base for humanity. Homogeneity is not interesting to life, and diversity of life forms is everywhere we look on Earth.

Do we really want a society where everyone thinks the same about everything? Clearly, humans are wired to be diverse, and so we should celebrate that. It is not that humans should be reined into some sort of "new religion" where everyone has exactly the same ideas and beliefs. However, we must consider a commonly shared worldview that enables diversity, creativity, and clear thinking—enabling people to share a flexible and sane worldview that is resonant with the most primary tunings of the universe.

In any society, as it develops technologically, there is a point at which everyone has the ability to pull the trigger and destroy everyone else. This much is inevitable. Divisiveness in terms of religious belief is then unthinkable. In this case, we have an obligation to ensure that all human beings are happy and content, that they have what they need, and are not so frustrated that they want to kill the rest of us or feel any need to gain power over us and control us. We need to look at these mechanisms in people who want to assume destruction, which pertain to thanatos or the will to power. We need to carefully guard all that we do and never become complacent, lest the forces that desire our destruction gain any foothold within our midst.

Assuming we collectively de-armor, become less calloused, and truly sensitive, our world would become magical and alive. Human tenderness would then become collectively possible, and the delicate nature of our inner world would be able to make contact with the inner and outer life of other people. We would then be at peace, living in a vast garden of plants, art, and technology. Food for the body, food for the soul, and food for the mind would be abundant. Each of us would be creating all of this nourishment for one other. That would be our true state—the state we were designed to live in—which is our true spiritual health and creative functionality.

As humanity flowers, there are stories and rhythms to be told of intricate adventures, which allow the magnificence of life to become apparent. Then we can choose to be motivated, to pollinate life, to create a vibrational field or electric atmosphere, and to live our own dreaming, and that of humanity, in an innate murmuration.

Humanity is evolving and will develop a new universal language, a global language, a global way of being, and, over time, we will evolve into a new species. What could have a greater priority for the architects of evolution than creating a foundation for this evolution to thrive upon? The old world has no more to offer. The old dramas are predictable. The stories have been played out. Whatever it is that a new heaven and a new earth promise, we must embrace it. To accept this embrace should not be difficult, but there are hurdles—such as truly accepting death in sweet surrender, to live again and resurrect life in its truest form.

Could we really do it ourselves?

There are some who say "the elite" of this world, meaning the wealthiest, and by proxy, most powerful people, already have designs to eliminate most of humanity. Some may wonder why they would want to do this. Perhaps this presumed "elite" perceive that it is "other people" ("Hell is other people"—French proverb) who make life disagreeable for them: traffic on the road, the pollution humanity creates, and the smelly masses getting in their way, inconveniencing their lifestyle.

The "conspiracy theory" rumor is that there are two methods already in progress: soft kill and hard kill[13]. Soft killing concerns the toxic and polluting elements that industrial societies appear to deliberately produce, eventually making most people infertile and unable to breed. Hard killing is said to be the elimination, the murder of billions, via deliberate and drastic measures, such as the release of a virus and a vaccine which renders billions infertile, or an even more unexpected tactic, such as the killing of the majority of people with drones and robots.

These are all very brutal and blunt solutions. Likely, only a supreme technology, of the kind that does not exist on Earth, could do the job of selectively choosing the RIGHT people to remain. This sort of technology could only arise from life forms that have highly advanced civilizations. Such an alien race would have technology that could instantly identify the people of most value to the human race. This alien race MUST have achieved a superior ethical, spiritual, and technological framework of development for them to be able to measure these qualities easily. Their level of development must be far beyond that of warfare, division, or money, and this transcendence of war means they will have developed the ultimate weapon: the ability to eliminate any biological life at will. This would also mean they would operate at a level far beyond more conflict driven alien races that may have more malevolent agendas. We would also hope that such an advanced race could protect humanity from such threats.

---

[13] "Hard kill" refers to overt, immediate methods of causing death or serious harm, such as wars, assassinations, or biological warfare. "Soft kill" involves more subtle, long-term methods of population control or harm, such as introducing toxins into food and water, using pharmaceuticals to induce chronic illness, or manipulating public perception through media. These concepts are generally considered by most to be "conspiracy theories," which suggest that powerful people are using these tactics to control or reduce populations.

Vanquishing has a ring to it

But how would this alien race vanquish the great majority of humanity? Perhaps they could carry out this culling through a kind of frequency, such as sound waves that could stop the heart. If they were to kill pretty much all human beings, how would they discriminate between those they want to kill and those they want to spare? Perhaps they would be able to transport the "desirables" away from Earth and then use a specific frequency to vanquish the remaining human beings. When the desirables were safely in craft above the Earth, the aliens could cause floods or other catastrophes, ensuring the deaths of all humans remaining on the planet. In that circumstance, such floods or other disasters would also kill the animals, leading us to believe that some sort of "Noah's Ark" would be required.

So how many people would be placed back on Earth? We have no way of knowing. Simply based upon my own intuitive calculations over a couple of decades, I would suggest 100 million is too many people and ten million is too little. Around 30 to 60 million people would likely be more than enough human beings to live on planet Earth. About 40 million people is 0.5% of the total population as of 2025. With a global population of 40 million people, it would also not be too hard to gather all the human beings on Earth in one place for important gatherings and meetings.

The end of industrial civilization is the beginning of human civilization

This team of humans left on Earth would then have to deal with the fallout from industrial civilization—immediate and long—term. Our impact upon the planet would have to be addressed, and the best tools and physical items recovered. Cleanup would begin, a process that could conceivably take decades. Then the real work would start: establishing a way of life that does not create waste, developing ways to grow optimal food, and socially organizing as a true tribe of humanity—all choosing to get along constructively as the most primary intention. We could begin to truly understand Earth's plant life, the source of all food and medicine, an understanding that current humans have only scratched the surface of, that would allow us to create the most desirable food and medicines for optimal health and well-being.

Most of all, we could understand ourselves and each other, creating a destiny where happiness, peace, and joy are baseline states for human existence. Maybe, finally, human life would not consist of so much suffering because we could truly evolve and live together in a functional and sincere manner. As a civilization, we would then be presentable to alien civilizations. As Team Humanity, we would all be able to focus on projects such as space travel without worrying about how much it costs. We could devote more time and resources to art—our highest expression of being. So many dreamers and visionaries have a myriad of ideas we could manifest. Our dreamers and visionaries could imagine a new world, so we could then dream a new world into existence.

CHAPTER 5: HOW WE COULD BE

Aftermath of choices

The event foretold in Middle Eastern religions as "Judgment Day," although beneficial to the planetary ecosystem, would nonetheless be absolutely heartbreaking for those humans who survived. Is there any way we could begin to understand their pain and loss? The sorrow and grief from literally losing everything would be immense. How long would it take for the survivors to recover from this loss and begin to organize collectively? We must consider how the survivors on Earth could organize a new way of life. How would they survive? How would they emotionally deal with the death of the greater majority of humanity? On a survival level, if less than one percent of the human population survived, they would have all the things they needed to function and survive—food, furniture, solar panels, cars, and tools.

The primary issue would be how such a society would socially organize and govern itself. Would such a society have elected leaders, such as a king or queen for the whole planet, or would decisions be made with the use of digital technology, without government? Would there be some sort of organized council, or all of the above: a king and queen, a council, and a direct form of intelligent direct democracy, all interrelating ideas and advice? Would the process of government be completely decentralized to a direct democracy, similar to the original Athenian democracy, where eligible citizens communicate and vote on relevant issues?

A new world would initially be based upon people simply surviving and sharing, and eventually, naturally transforming into a marketplace-based system with a type of centralized global currency. A centralized global currency isn't necessarily to be shunned at all, provided it is free of corruption, control, and the negative issues that currencies have in our world. These issues may include inflation, usury, and all the unnecessary complexities of the financial sector, such as foreign exchange and the stock market. Perhaps the value of such a global currency could be equated to the number of humans on the planet, the extant amount of resources human beings circulate, as well as the amount of productive work they should optimally carry out each year. Rather than having the backing of gold or other metals, such a currency could be backed by human beings, the amount of metals on Earth, and the productive output of human beings. This global human currency would ideally have relative stability. The purpose of society is then not to create more currency or more resources, but to better the human quality of life. Eventually, it might be possible to measure quality of life—or what is most meaningful for human beings—and coordinate these values to currency.

Any form of investing or profiting from financial manipulations (which are entrenched parts of our world) would no longer be necessary in a sane world not motivated by greed and scarcity. Perhaps a new system could provide new tokens of value, representing human output of effort, energy and creativity. Perhaps there are forms of currency we share with each other personally. Perhaps there could be forms of currency that reward excellence and high achievement. In this way, we could "gamify" many aspects of human life in order to encourage people and highlight for everyone what is most "noteworthy" within society.

The most primary issue with "capitalism" is greed, whereby companies and individuals operate for "profit." It is easy to see that by eliminating the profit motive, society could operate very effectively, as people would be simply incentivized to work for their own benefit. The more effectively they work and the more value they provide, the more they would be rewarded. In a fair society, everyone would get a chance to be highly rewarded for their work, not just owners of companies and those who can afford to invest in the stock market.

Quality over quantity

Perhaps the most important aspect of a drastic reduction in human population is that the plant, insect, and animal species would regain their natural habitat. We should give planet Earth back almost all of the arable land designated for unsustainable agriculture, to let it grow wild and regenerate into its own form, free of human interference. Let the land rest, and let the plants and animals come back. Perhaps this must be our primary work as a species—to allow the ecology of the planet to return to balance after many hundreds of years of ecological terrorism, caused by our explosive population growth. This does not need to be a sacrifice or a limitation on how human beings behave and live, as so-called "eco-fascists" believe, such as Finnish ecologist and author Pentti Linkola. Human beings can live optimally in harmony with nature while using natural resources, as long as we are not dominating and spoiling the natural resources of Earth.

Some people may say that if we reduce the human population so drastically, it will lessen the impact of our civilization, and we will not be able to do the things we previously did, such as constructing buildings, bridges, or roads. Yet it actually takes relatively few people to carry out these sorts of projects. If anything, in a highly mobilized, efficient society without capital constraints, humanity would be able to embark upon much bigger engineering projects than ever before, as "cost" would not present an issue. Then, many large projects would only require people willing to embark upon the work involved.

Our present system is opposed to giving everyone what they need, as the entire system is based on scarcity and keeping people motivated to do things they do not want to do. To mass-produce typically means to cut corners and create inferior items designed to break. At present, it is inconvenient and costly to manufacture most items to be biodegradable, so there is little impetus to make things as they should rightfully be made if we were truly conscientious. There is not much motivation in government or corporations to stop producing so much rubbish, as doing so would cut profits. Therefore, we create enormous amounts of appalling and inexcusable waste, all the while producing emissions that restrict our breathing. Trash is only symbolic of consumer convenience, and we are, in a sense, cursing space (and ourselves) by filling it with non-compostable, discarded materials. In a sane society, wasteful packaging would not be required. Besides, everything can be recycled.

Creating a space for yourself

The potential life we could experience together as a species in an optimally functioning civilization would far exceed the lifestyles of the richest people today who are living "optimally." There would be many opportunities in such a culture for growing, for being recognized, for learning, and for contributing to a rich social tapestry whereby people are enjoying themselves. This would not be a lifestyle based around comfort or luxury; instead, people would be focused on growing and learning about themselves and others. In a society already committed to high quality, there would not be areas where a lack of quality of things is an issue and so "luxury" becomes redundant as a concept. There is only what is optimal and reasonable in terms of how material resources are used, depending on the outcome. Such a lifestyle would involve profound forms of aesthetic, artistic, interpersonal, and human enjoyment.

In a global civilization with a small population, there would be space for everyone to live where they wish. You would be able to create your own space anywhere, as there would be no scarcity of land. Sure, many people may want a sea view, and with a greatly reduced population, everyone could live by the sea if that's what they want. In this way of life, individuals could take care of land and buildings (which is a responsibility) that fulfills what custodianship really means. Individuals can only caretake land; it cannot be owned, as this is an artificial figure of speech that promotes unhealthy living. Ultimately, people want to live near their friends, family, and community, rather than by themselves with a sea view—though that is what some people might well want.

No scarcity

We think that money motivates, but only begrudgingly, because we often don't like our work. If we are to be rewarded, we don't need a system of reward; rewards can be spontaneous. We reward, and we are rewarded, based upon assertions of merit. More than reward, human beings require not just respect, but acknowledgment for their contribution to society. We need to make society both interesting and novel, stimulating and relaxed. Money is not a true measure of a good life. A good life involves growth, friends, challenge, connection, learning, and adventure, not the trimmings and tailings. We should stop giving oxygen to this arcane, survival-based paradigm of gold and gems, and cease perpetuating the idea that the trimmings and tailings have any necessary value at all.

Gazette

We would also need to create a standardized form of global social media. In a way, our new internet must at once be autonomous and incorruptible. The structures of social media and the internet would become intertwined with forms of exchange and how we work together and make collective decisions. As such, our new form of internet would become the primary way in which we act and move through society.

Some may wonder if we really will need a new system at all in a new world, when systems appear only necessary for people who cannot self-govern—for those who cannot think for themselves. An enlightened society would create and replace systems as they needed them, in a similar way to how we use the internet. Applications and websites become popular and then become redundant; operating systems and protocols come and go, to be used when we need them. We rule them—they do not rule us. That's a big difference. Think of the really clever people you know. Do they necessarily need or want systems? No, they are always very flexible. Systems are tools for them; they are not ruled by systems, and they often make their own.

If you were to hypothetically create a new system for living on our planet that was truly aligned with human values, it is likely that the majority of people we currently have on Earth would corrupt it with their greed, ineptness, and selfishness. They would also likely break the rules of the system to suit their whims and interpersonal politics. Their motivations are often too selfish and unaligned with the well-being of humanity as a whole.

The purpose of an open-source civilization with flexible systems is to bring people back to what the American psychologist Abraham Maslow called self-actualization[14]. Once people have their fundamental needs met, they will generally focus on actualizing themselves and fulfilling their potential to grow, to relate with each other, and to focus on what is most important as human beings. It is a truly human imperative to create systems that support an individual's growth and the overall psychic health of humanity. To that end, we must inculcate within such systems mentors, advisors, and other individuals who can support each person in their life and growth. This is one thing clearly missing in our capitalistic society—the innate support and encouragement of a greater community built within the structure of how such a human-focused culture would surely operate.

People commonly look for some golden structure or new system that can be lived by. In fact, as humans grow and evolve, their structures and systems need to change and adapt. Any civilization that cannot evolve its own systems to suit the needs of its people is not worth its salt. Our civilization is clearly not worth its salt, and if it is not worth its salt, then it must be destroyed to make way for a better way. We need to be flexible, not enslaved to one way, as this posits a system as an answer, rather than human intelligence, creativity, or ingenuity.

There are many possibilities for new systems, but

---

[14] Abraham Maslow was an American psychologist from the last century, most famous for his "hierarchy of human needs." Depicted as a pyramid, at the bottom are basic needs—food, water, warmth, shelter, and safety. Then follows psychological needs, intimate relationships, friendship, feelings of accomplishment. Finally comes self-fulfillment needs—actualizing one's highest potential and forming a resounding view of oneself, which comes at the top of pyramid. Any sane society would be based upon allowing individuals to fulfill these needs. Needs on the lower end of the pyramid have to be fulfilled before an individual can realize needs higher on the pyramid. Abraham Maslow toward the end of his life placed transcendence at the top of the pyramid, rather than self-actualization.

"Transcendence refers to the very highest and most inclusive or holistic levels of human consciousness, behaving and relating, as ends rather than means, to oneself, to significant others, to human beings in general, to other species, to nature, and to the cosmos."

perhaps what we need to do is test and utilize various systems to be very flexible about what is created in different areas of the planet. The most essential and true system is common sense and human intelligence. In a world where people's connection to common sense has often become atrophied from following insane systems and rules, many cannot see how this internal sense could be a guiding force. But if we lived in a population of people who had common sense and were truly connected to their own intelligence, and operated in a framework of communicative, self-correcting awareness, this would actually be quite straightforward.

What is most vital is that we create systems that facilitate people's growth so that we can do better at whatever we are doing through constructive feedback and advice. An open-source civilization can enable others to comment, critique, and give advice and suggestions. This is what is often missing in governments and corporations. So many of us have problems with bureaucracy, but who do we tell to make a difference? At what point will a difference actually be made? Furthermore, what incentives in our society are there to sit down and write a letter to your local parliamentarian or corporate CEO, which may not even be read or taken seriously?

In a sane society, everyone would be satiated materially and have enough food and shelter in which to survive. When individuals have everything they need and are secure in their physical existence, they can engage more deeply in their own growth and well-being and be able to share more freely with others the essence of who they are. People can then realize their primary need for human connection and the consequent need to bring value to the table and learn how to truly interact and relate with others in a cooperative capacity.

When we are no longer compelled to scamper around just to survive, when we can relax and know that we will survive—then it becomes only a matter of exchanging energy and skills for what we need to thrive. A world where people cannot even get a job in order to survive is seriously ill. That is an unfortunate and crazy situation that too many people find themselves in. In a sane society, you should always be able to exchange your time and energy to get what you need to survive at any time. That is only fair and just.

Moreover, everyone should have access to a residence, a vehicle, comfortable furniture, and land. Upon arriving on spaceship Earth, you should be entitled to access these basic implements in order to make a life. Without them, you would struggle, often living your whole life in order to access these things. We must remove this struggle to survive, and collectively evolve into a state of being beyond survival. Most people in the world today never get to own their own home, car, motorcycle, or even a bicycle. Probably, in a sane society, transport would be abundant. There would be plenty of cars, motorcycles, bicycles, planes, and other flying objects you could hire and use to travel wherever you wish. This is freedom. How we live now, enmeshed in time and space on Earth, is not freedom, and to meet a truly free person is very rare indeed.

If every human being had access to land, then food would become less of an issue. Housing materials and other raw materials would be already extant. How many more trees would we need to cut down, and how many more miles of road would we need to build? As a species, we would have mined enough and wouldn't need to cut down more trees to provide housing for 50 to 100 million people. More than one billion houses already exist. Good furniture for millions of people already exists. We could also each produce these things for ourselves, given the equipment and know-how.

The meaning of work

Our cultural understandings are so based upon being "paid" and "rewarded" in money that we have lost sight of other types of reward. Money enmeshes all of us so much that we have lost sight of what we really want and how to get it. As individuals, we can only drive one car at a time, live in one house, and sit on one chair. Once our nest is furnished, we must live within it. The more items we own, the more responsible we must be for them. There is no question that healthy food is good, and comfortable furniture and bedding are not evil things. Once we have attained these things and they are of sufficient quality, we shouldn't be compelled by greed to get more things to merely feather our nest.

While trying to get more money to buy a better car or a holiday house, people are enslaved by desire. Society would do well to discourage desire, as religions typically do, instead of encouraging or motivating people's activities through consumerism. Money, for its own sake, is only ever a means to an end. Money symbolizes status, freedom, quality, pleasure, and fulfilment, but does not necessarily bring these factors from what we can purchase. The sad thing is that those with money often do not know how to utilize it for the benefit of others beyond themselves. Philanthropy and charity are clearly worthwhile, but do not tend to truly evolve the human situation.

Hopefully, a society such as the one considered here would not create individuals with entitled "rich kid" syndrome—where people live in a kind of existential malaise with nothing to do or be. The rich kid syndrome only exists because, without playing the money game, such people often don't know what to do with themselves, as there are few fulfilling environments in the world that do not relate to accumulating money. If you take the money game out of the equation and only give people the option of actualizing their potential—truly enmeshed in growing as human beings—then their own actualization would be their overall focus. For example, a chef cooks because he loves to cook. To do so to the best of his potential is his passion. To have the acclaim and appreciation of other human beings is the icing on the cake. If you really do love to cook, it makes sense for you to be a chef and do that work—to grow and learn how to become a better chef.

Every person is born with certain talents and abilities. For most people, few of these qualities are fully harnessed. In our society, people learn to compromise within the often severe functional limits of the workplace and their jobs. Even in a system not bound by sales in the marketplace, success is essentially determined by how many people want to actually engage with your creations. Sure, not everyone is a good writer, and not all are destined to be read by many people. Clearly, we should make all work so intrinsically rewarding and interesting that everyone would want to be involved. Society is then like a big to-do list, with organizations of people choosing and putting forward projects that could be undertaken.

In a sustainable society, we would require people to garden and grow food, to build houses, to create art and objects, to create technology, and to carry out scientific research. Furthermore, we would want people to understand the human organism and other animals, applying science in its truest possible sense. Science itself needs to evolve and transform into an open-source, flexible, explorative, multimedia creation. We would then always need to ask, "How can we do things better? How can we truly grow and evolve most effectively?"

We can get an idea of how people could propose action in a new society via how crowdfunding occurs now. In our world, an idea is presented to everyone through a digital medium; people offer their money to support the idea, and the more people who support it, the more likely it will be funded. In a sane society, where accumulation of money is not the primary objective, you would contribute your time toward such a project, you could contribute your feedback, and help "vote" such projects into existence. Instead of having to buy tools or materials you need for your project, you could borrow tools from a tool bank. The only things you need is people and their time to make your project happen.

We need to think about tangible incentives beyond intrinsic rewards. How would we motivate human beings if not via money? Would that incentive be the chance to drive the latest, most extravagant cars? Is it the time of a distinguished elder or a skillful masseur? Is it access to beautiful houses or special parties? What is it that people will truly want? Will they truly want for anything—or will they be happy just to be, to live in such a society and create their own lifestyle and their own destiny?

Capitalism is based on a kind of slavery—of "others" doing the work for you, while the owners of the company reap the presumed rewards. All services rendered for money represent a kind of prostitution, where actions are created out of force and not innately imbued with meaning. In a system that does not truly allow love to make the world go around, those who have no love would surely starve and therefore may fear dying if the world were run according to what are, perhaps, something like its own innate rules.

We must reduce work hours to fewer than 40 hours a week—to something like 10 to 20 hours. Then, work would be done effortlessly and passionately, having been invigorated by other activities. People need to work, or they will lack aim and passion. Yet to make work the center of human life is to miss out on the purpose of being alive, which is to live—to be present to ourselves and other people, experience the culture that other human beings create and to enjoy the dance of life.

In a sane society, there could be quotas of necessary work and a registration of work hours in a digital registry. If you were able to work wherever you traveled, your time in these places could be far more rewarding than if you traveled without working or contributing. Even those who are working as rocket scientists on time-sensitive projects would probably work better under a 20 hour maximum workweek and could work wherever they desire.

If humanity is to live as a global society, we would want to release human beings from having to live in one place or work in unnecessary roles. Perhaps individuals should be encouraged to work two to four hours a day, which would leave plenty of time for learning or play, recreational activities, friendships, and relationships. As it stands, our system trains and tailors people over many years, leaving them largely stuck within a "job." But it would be better if people could choose where they work and be flexible about what work they do. With fewer work hours, people could be trained in so many more fields and therefore be qualified to do so many more things, if that is their aim.

If you do not love what you do, then you clearly should not be doing it. Working for money is ultimately not a valid motivation. In a society that truly respects the time of the individual, what would happen to the jobs that nobody really wants to do? Many things can be done in ways that minimize labour. There are always solutions to problems of unnecessary work, and people will enjoy solving such problems. As we are beginning to see now, humanity is emerging into the usage of artificial intelligence and the use of robots, so that most of what we presently know as work can be automated.

In many cultures, sharing is a habit. Jobs that have to be done should be delegated. There are always things that need to be repaired, things that need to be cleaned and maintained. People will commonly ask, in regard to the proposition of a utopia, "Who will take out the trash? Who will clean the streets?" Perhaps the least desirable and simplest jobs requiring the most labor can be given to young people. As they progress in their learning, they would master how to do even simple and straightforward tasks with proficiency. It is not that we should be creating a culture of no work. However, Western culture values "overwork"—work for its own sake— and money for its own sake. In a truly global village, we should be prioritizing what matters most to us. Time is the most precious thing we have, so why should we continue to waste so much of it on unnecessary toil?

Different skills take different amounts of time to learn. Obviously, doctors and surgeons spend a great deal of time learning their craft. When people are only required to work for a relatively small number of hours, people will want to work and contribute. They will want to share their talents. Life would become a sharing, and each of us would be recognized for the work we share with our community and our species on our social media.

What about those people who choose not to work? If you are not working, presumably there are reasons why. Perhaps you have fallen in love and want to spend more time with your lover. In a sane society, everyone would see and understand that. Other people may even be more inspired in their work if they have fallen in love.

Work becomes much less necessary as a primary focus when society chooses not to make full-time work necessary. Shorter working house mean that people will work more vigorously and effectively. Should we stop those who want to pursue difficult problems and work 18 hours a day? Perhaps not—but we should probably guide them to find leisure and community, to bring them back into enjoyment and presence, instead of rewarding them excessively by encouraging their "work addiction."

In a highly intelligent, mobile society, there would be many more people reaching their potential, so rocket scientists who may be indispensable now would become more commonplace. People can become negatively consumed by the passion they have for their work, so we need to bring them back to essential productivity—back to their humanity, to deeper reasons and meanings for their existence beyond their productive output.

It is of vital importance that people spend time "living" and being involved in relatively unproductive actions involving mutual care, communion, and communication. Then the productive work people do becomes more effective and not strained or stressed, and creativity, problem-solving, and efficiency are optimized.

If work is made innately fun, with intrinsic rewards and challenges, then people will want to do it. Moreover, people can create their own work. If there are elements or structures that people deem desirable to exist in a society, it should be possible for individuals and groups to easily create them. Such endeavours that improve people's lives also improve the individual's résumé.

In an ideal situation, there is no need for "jobs," only roles that come and go as needed. The aim of our current civilization is to create "more jobs" and create work for people, no matter what the quality of work is, requiring people to carry out often very unpleasant and meaningless tasks. In a sane civilization, on the other hand, the aim is to create as little work as possible—only what's necessary for the optimum functioning of a society—and to maximize the time people can give to learning, leisure, being with loved ones, and other forms of playing and being that we cannot even conceive of in our current civilization. This is the future of the optimal human being, not fusing our consciousness to circuit boards or transferring our being to silicon processors. The way forward for flesh and blood humans is activating and living our primary spiritual nature and, therefore, just being happy.

CHAPTER 6: AN OPTIMAL SOCIETY FOR ALL HUMAN BEINGS

The basis of a new system

In this day and age, many people directly recognize that humanity is one species—essentially even one being, experiencing itself through all of us. The expression and life of that being are severely hampered by the present genetic nature of humanity and the environment we have created. What is that genetic nature, and how was that genetic nature brought into existence? How was it shaped, and by what forces? We know that all these people are present in such plague proportions because of sexual intercourse and better standards of living. Humanity is clearly not able to adequately express itself through most of these people and the environment they are living in.

The collective actions of a society need to arise from the collective will of that society, not from mechanical imperatives. This collective is nuanced and multifaceted. There is largely no will, conscience, or true humanity in how corporations act, as they are merely extensions of human greed and the desire to grow bigger and accumulate more. Capitalism clearly exploits the human desire to accumulate wealth, and that is how people are expected to be motivated—to accumulate and grow their money. In most societies, this is how status is conferred: through the amount of money accumulated by individuals. In reality, it is only the few people at the top of the financial ladder who get the opportunity to accumulate much money, and the masses are effectively treated as "wage slaves" in our society.

Even though this system makes some sense to many of us (especially those oriented in such a way to exploit the system), it isn't actually a very good way to run a society. It only truly benefits a small number of people who may be savvy enough or have enough surplus income to spend their time investing in the stock market. Communism, as a perceived alternative system, is clearly not a very sophisticated or human-oriented model, not taking into account human nature and how people are motivated and incentivized to act in this world.

If society were structured so that individuals increased their status through the quality of their efforts, we would have a very effective incentive as a basis for making a society work. Then it becomes a matter of how we create and tinker the game, so people can improve their lot—and everyone can see what their LOT is. This could tie in with a centralized and incorruptible social media called Gazette, which records your work and study efforts. If all of our efforts and activities were recorded in an open book, in many respects, this would be incentive enough.

Many resist the idea of some sort of gamified society or social credit system because they know that within a tyranny, such a system is going to be rigged against them and punish them for pushing back against the tyranny. However, if we lived in a non-tyrannical society for the benefit of human beings, then that system would assist us to play the game of life. The system would be like any good video game—one that we would all have to agree is fair, even though it may be difficult at times. The gamification of society is just a society with appropriate rewards, checks, and balances. Human beings are clearly motivated more by rewards (like dolphins are) than by punishments.

We must appreciate that our society is already "gamified." It is just that this game is very limited, largely rigged, unfair, and working against almost all of us. The present game we are playing offers limited rewards and incentives, is inefficient, and doesn't provide positive outcomes for most people.

Society as a whole should always be calibrating the direction of its ethos—what it values, what qualities it develops within its citizens—and then allowing the creation of these faculties. In a non-tyrannical society, the government would have to become a transparent, open-source medium rather than a mechanism to enforce rules or power over people.

A society that works for the benefit of the human being is an alien concept to many and may seem utopian, but actually is the only logical and sensible choice for a sane society that works for the benefit of its members.

Humanity is clearly not at an evolutionary stage where we can let go of currency, as we still need to measure and understand how our efforts and time are utilized. The issue is that society has created a bunch of insecure hoarders because society has decided that access to resources is the name of the game of survival. In a sane society unhooked from the survival imperative, our status should be measured more by how we have developed ourselves spiritually, the level of our humanity, or by what we have actually achieved as human beings in terms of what we have created and contributed to society.

Money should be perceived simply as a medium of exchange, perhaps more like a lubricant than a fuel. It shouldn't even be amounts of fuel that determine what a society does and how it does it. Society should do what it wants to do. There should be no effective limits to what we can do and what projects we choose to pursue. Our only effective limits exist in the amount of people who have the time to contribute to certain projects.

It could be a human possibility to transcend currency, but in order to make society function effectively, a global currency appears necessary. The issue with our system is that due to all the profiteering, currency becomes corrupted and exploited. A global stable currency that doesn't inflate or deflate, based upon all the truest values in the world makes a great deal of sense.

One way to create an equitable and sensible system would be to convert all companies into non-profit organizations. That means all profits should simply go back into the company's range of activities or be given back to society, chosen by those working in the company, rather than money going to shareholders or owners, or even people working for that company. This means that taxation would no longer necessary because the people working within the organization can choose where their money goes, instead of the government choosing where it goes. Salaries earned from working at the company enable people to make a living and buy things they need to support their lives. People could take out interest—free loans to buy the things they need that cost larger amounts of money, but not be strangled by these loans, as so many people in our current society are by their credit cards or house loans.

Clearly, the income tax rate of 30-60 percent in many countries is blatant theft. Most of us around the world get very little for what we pay in tax. Individuals shouldn't have to pay tax—only organizations and companies. A society of intelligent and efficient people is not likely to create a bureaucratic class and a culture of red tape and regulations, so basic services like hospitals, ambulances, schools, roads, and various spaces of the commons shouldn't actually cost very much. A culture of independent and conscious people is not liable to be regulated and do not need to have so many rules applied to them. For sure a society needs to have some rules—without the rules, there is no game. There still needs to be enforcers of the rules, such as law enforcement and courts, but a one-world global culture would not require militaries anymore. People living in a system that is not tyrannical, and who are not living among dangerous and desperate people, would no longer need weapons to defend themselves. A global culture may need to think about how to defend itself from intergalactic threats rather than from members of the human species.

Humanity must resist the tendency toward polarization and dualistic tribalism, and recognize these as an outdated mode of being determined by tyranny. A divided world of one group of people going in one direction and a group of people going in another is not the way to run a country or a global human tribe, and neither is creating two countries on Earth at all sane.

We must consider a new human civilization—one tolerant of those who want to live in the way they wish. For example, in the United States, the Amish are largely free to live how they wish to live. Few Amish leave their community and join a corrupted society devoid of spiritual values. An uncorrupted society would be one in which the Amish can feel they fit into and not compromise their values. Could we envision a society with enough community and spiritual values that the Amish decide they all want to take part? This is the challenge—not to seduce people, but to create a global society so enriching and rewarding that everyone would want to take part. Ideally, this society would be so inspirational that it would become addictive. It would bring people to states of being where they are firing on all cylinders, and the effects of recreational drugs would pale in comparison to people's spiritual state of being.

My company is your company

Companies and organizations begin when people come together to fulfill a demand or begin something new. The basic positions are filled, and the plans are submitted to Gazette. Then the currency required to start the project could be unlocked from a central bank when enough people willing to work are brought together. Not all projects are voted on or manifested into existence. There may be compelling arguments why such a project shouldn't exist or is not necessary. All these issues can be debated and voted upon.

Without people owning companies, we would prevent billionaires from even existing. Then people would be limited as to how much money they could make, and the pursuit of money for its own sake would be automatically limited. We would manufacture the game of society so that there are innate limits on how much money you could accumulate and how much money you could spend.

If you are in the top ten percent of "achievers" within society, then you should be able to have the resources to build or buy a big house. If you were in the top one percent, perhaps you could have access to a private jet. In a sane society that used resources consciously, you wouldn't have your own pilot and jet, which you might only fly 300 hours a year. If your role in society really needed you to access a private jet (and you had a profile that demanded a certain level of privacy), you could be given access to a network of private jets. Perhaps there might be fewer than 100 people bestowed access to their own private jet.

Ideally, we want to create an ethos in the culture where people are not valued for their monetary worth or the mere numbers in their bank account, but actually by what contributions they make to society. People's contributions may be as an artist, a problem solver, a seer, a creator of new projects, or as a visionary leader or mediator. The status of a person in a sane society is defined by what they do for their friends and how they carry themselves in that doing.

We do need to value and reward the most esteemed people in society. What we don't want is the ultra-wealthy throwing around their wealth and power, wasting resources, owning 20 houses that remain empty, while many people are left out in the cold. The people we want at the top are the most responsible, careful, and conscious people, not just the people who are most useful to the current tyranny.

In a sane society where basic needs are straightforward, people would not be scurrying around to buy things as a personal priority. A sane society should draw people away from possessions, away from their toys, and into a field of being useful to other people, animals, and the environment around them.

Senior members of society should make more money than junior members, but it shouldn't be more than 10–20 times what a junior member makes. People with more aptitude should be more incentivized. Having nice things is an incentive, but it should not be the primary incentive that makes people move within a conscious society. If we were a truly functional society, people would be moved by love, and some things wouldn't have prices on them. Some things would be considered sacred and given as rewards for great work and acts of being and service.

The intention of the game of society is to challenge people—to get them to show up, give their best, and help them grow and evolve—without ignoring that there is an innate competitive nature to human beings. Perhaps we cannot deny social credit; perhaps there is no true hiding our strengths and weaknesses, and if we want to live in an honest and transparent society, who we really are and how we act needs to be on the table. If we are to be accountable for our strengths and weaknesses to a wider community, then at least we have a foundation with which to address our mutual reality.

The game of accumulating the most money is rather boring compared to all the games we could play. It does not take into account the human need to grow, show up, and be themselves in creativity. If we lived in a high-trust society, we would only need one social media channel—called Gazette—which would be connected to our forms of currency, and the way we can participate in a true democracy and make decisions about our society. Through this medium, we could communicate and give feedback to each other and our systems. Through honest, kind, and useful feedback, we can grow and improve whatever it is we are doing. Whereas within our unfair and rigged systems, a rating of 3.7 out of 5 stars is mostly terrible, and when we give low feedback, we are often punishing someone's livelihood.

If we lived in a society that created an equitable culture in which excess accumulation was effectively prevented, it would be a logical society that highlights the illogical senselessness of capitalistic culture. We all know the supermarket and big banks do not need our money or do much useful with it. Yet, almost all our money goes to these corporations—and not into the hands of the people who actually need it. This is not a sane use of human energy, especially while people are starving and suffering because they don't have enough.

We need to envision a society where people use their energy to do what they want and have the freedom to engage their own dreaming. In our society, money promises that, but the wealthy more often than not don't have as much freedom to do as they wish. After buying all the obvious high-ticket items, like fast cars and big houses, there is little they can do to improve their lot in a real and human sense. Of course, 99.9 percent of people don't know that being able to buy anything you want does not make you happy. They are still enslaved by the game itself and the hope that one day they will be wealthy. In a sane society, we would see excessive accumulation not as the barometer of a person's value, but as a reflection of their spiritual development—their capacity to love, to deal with difficult situations, to communicate and be helpful to others, to create beauty, and to contribute meaning to the human world.

If we lived in a society devoted to creating spaces and activities you would want to engage with—where money will not buy you entry—you would earn access through developing and growing your own character and aptitude in being a human. Most of all, people want to be recognized and held in high esteem by others. Creating a culture and "game" of society whereby people are able to show who they are, we can motivate them to be their best.

An environment we choose

We need to ask ourselves, "What is the ideal environment for human beings to live in? And what are the primary needs of human beings? What is it that human beings need to DO?" Clearly, our technologies are making us redundant for most of the things we previously did, and our present model of society, based around the marketplace, is not spiritually sustaining for human beings.

Human beings have traditionally lived in tribal groups as a default way of life. Atomized people of industrial civilization typically find this type of group intimacy very challenging, yet perhaps it is the key challenge we need to devote ourselves to. Our human nervous systems are nurtured by the feedback and energy of other human beings. In order to grow, we need to feel the love, support, and admonition—the FEEDBACK—of other human beings.

There is a deep need to be able to enter into intimacy with other human beings. Our society highlights fleshy sex as the primary arena of intimacy, but a culture based around pseudo-procreative sex as the goalpost is going to miss the mark. Most human beings could agree that love and connection are the purpose of intimacy, even within sex. An intelligent society could allow us to meet and engage with others in deep human intimacy, whereas our society and "the apps" leave us to fend for ourselves in a rigged and oversexualised game with very few winners.

Human beings ideally need to do things together. The question to ask is what there is to do when our technologies are increasingly able to do so much—even create art. People clearly do have a need to work alongside others on common goals.

Play is also important, and as we evolve, our games and the ways we play and live will change, too. Human beings need a sense of challenge, resistance, and something to overcome. It may well be that what we create in terms of games, not video games, but real-life games, will represent the physical, emotional, and mental challenges that truly test who we are.

Group discussion and dialogue are also a significant part of being a human and something that takes time. A sane society would allow us the time to cultivate our relationships with our community, children, parents, friends, and partners—but also give us time for quiet reflection and deep consideration in peace.

Many people need an edge, a challenge, even a danger—and this is why men have traditionally gone to war. Modern society often lacks such an edge or danger, hence why many seek extreme sports or physical challenges. Also, such an edge or exploration of these edges we can constructively use to our collective advantage. Warfare has become redundant as an arena where people could be tested on all levels, as technology has largely taken over warfare, leaving people without a true challenge. New types of games and sports that have an edge to them could replace warfare. We need to keep in mind that the dangers of the natural world and warfare would naturally cull those who made severe mistakes, so nature takes them out of the gene pool.

To be a sustainable society, we need to naturally improve our genetics, and the primary way to improve our genetics is to prune the least able among us. If we can find a way to create an edge in our society so that the bottom one percent in overall performance would have to permanently leave the human tribe, we could ensure that, over generations, there are no elements that drag humanity down.

If you are consistently in the bottom one percent of everything you do in a society, chances are that life is not going to be very satisfactory for you anyway. The threat of being in the bottom one percent would inspire everyone to perform at a higher level. Any kind of collective society must have mechanisms within it where it is not possible to coast along and be indolent and lazy.

If you are indolent, lazy, and not fit or able, a sane society will ensure you fall off a cliff. That doesn't mean you have to be punished, but growing up in such a society you will see and know people who don't make it. Being in such a society is a privilege, not a right; you must be initiated into it. Some will fail the initiation. The initiation shouldn't be so hard that ten percent fail and do not make it. This doesn't mean we should do anything inhumane, but within the understanding that death is not the ultimate end, the fallout from these initiations somehow becomes bearable.

In a completely sterile society where people do not face death, they lose an element of their edge—their humanness. Death within society also causes us to reflect on our lives.

This does not mean that if you cannot run a marathon in two hours, you would meet the chipper head-on. Some people cannot run a marathon but can do other things to a high degree. Those who are not putting in the effort and lack the overall qualities necessary to make a decent life will not make it.

For those in the bottom five percent, they will need to up their game in order to avoid the chop. At a certain point in one's life—say after the age of 25—this no longer becomes a threat, as you will have passed the required initiations to become a full member of society.

Not wanting to be a member of this global tribe would be unthinkable to most, simply because the potential and sheer fun of it would be too appealing. So what about people who don't want to take the risk of going through all these initiations and just want to be left alone and live in isolation? Are there snowy and rocky places where they can live away from everything and from everyone in a global human society? Sure there are. We cannot force everyone to participate in society with its inherent rules, and we certainly have people like this in our present, unfair society who are mostly harmless. Ideally, you want to make society fair and humane so everyone wants to participate. If people start protesting about society and how unfair it is, society itself needs to listen, collectively consider, and be able to change if necessary. A sane society is flexible and can give everyone a role based on their own personal needs and requirements.

A conscious society itself must inherently align with spiritual evolutionary potentials, which we presently do not yet fully understand. It would mean that we can collectively merge into a kind of conscious dreaming. We need to perceive "enlightenment" not just as a phenomenon of one individual. After all, can one enlightened person truly live in an unenlightened society? The most essential illumination or flowering of humanity is innately a collective phenomenon. We would then become involved in a kind of dreaming—a metaphysical presence—where we are developing fields of energy and beingness that we might presently, rather weakly, call "atmosphere," "vibe," or "love." Yet these emanations are clearly a major part of our primary reason for being human in the first place.

Society also needs to be fun—not just superficially playful, but a place in which we truly want to live. Fun involves challenges and achievement, social connection, novelty and surprise, and having the ability to create or have a sense of agency or power. In a sane society, we would be able to delegate and share power rather than leaving it to people who may misuse that power and only seek it for its own sake over us. Perhaps then human life would not appear to us to be one of such suffering.

CHAPTER 7: WE SHOULD ALL JUST GET ALONG

The meaning of community

Relationship is clearly the highest value we have as human beings, and this is also the primary element we possess that AI doesn't. In Western culture, people have largely lost the ability to devote time to one another compared to tribal societies. Perhaps the most worthwhile thing we can do is create friendships and spend quality time with friends and family. But often, work takes over, and we have no time for the ones we love or for being with others with whom we could have loving relationships. Many people already see these relationships as primary—as should any sane society. It is by spending time with one another that we form relationships, and this time is the most precious thing we have.

If we look at highly evolved sea mammals with brains larger than ours, such as orcas, dolphins, and whales, their entire lives are largely social. They communicate through different mediums, such as song, sonar, and telepathy, and live their lives in social groups. The meaning of their lives appears to be scripted in dynamic interrelation with one another, in a way humans cannot fully understand. If you get a chance to observe indigenous people, you will see that the bonds between them are very strong because there are few distractions to focus on apart from one another. They can spend large amounts of time in group discussions or involve themselves in elaborate rituals. In tribal societies, people innately devote time to one another. Their interpersonal skills and ability to communicate and live with one another in relative harmony give them a shared strength that highly individualized Western people typically lack.

There is a timelessness, a field, a mood, a momentum—a most essential atmosphere—that a group of people create when they are together in a meaningful community. Advertisements commonly show young people in swimming pools, frolicking together. How important is frolicking to our health? Frolicking may well be one of the most significant and overlooked elements in which to enable human well-being. Perhaps our entire society needs to be inspired and oriented toward creating frolicking as a key factor, which will inspire a deep sense of belonging, gratitude, and love in the human heart.

Dealing with anti-sociality

If we consider what the most optimal way for human beings to live might be, there certainly are some questions involved. Is suburban living the best way? Do we stay with the nuclear family? Is marital fidelity really the best for all? Do some people need to engage with many partners sexually in order to grow in a human and spiritual sense? What are the conditions—external and internal—for creating love? How do we make ourselves temples for the gods and goddesses to appear and dance within us? How can we share the raising of children? How much of the time should we be enjoying life, resting, or engaging in play?

Though the answers to these questions are likely to be different for each person, we need to create a bespoke civilization that meets the human and spiritual needs of different people. A truly free society allows everyone to live the life that is in their best interest, as long as they are not impinging upon others. A truly free society allows individuals who have innate guidance systems to create a life for their own best interests and also for that of human society. Yes, there should be many options—curricula or job positions—none of which are forced upon you.

If we lived in a society where the tendencies toward anti-sociality had largely been weeded out because human beings in that society had been preselected for their proactivity and ability to create life and culture, we wouldn't have to worry about renegade terrorist cells developing or need to create a whole bunch of rules for people. We underestimate how well-behaved many human cultures are in our world. The Japanese and the Finns, for example, have a self-correcting level of equanimity, safety, and civility that many other cultures would find difficult to emulate.

Conscious and aware people who are connected to their own kin will tend to naturally self-correct if they err. A communicative society of people who actually care for one another would support other people to find equanimity in their lives. If we have a society of conscious and self-aware people, a lot of rules would likely not be as necessary as they are in our world. People with a conscience and empathy generally tend to want to do the right thing. Doing the "wrong thing" is something that only children and teenagers do, as they test boundaries and discover the consequences of their actions. If we lived in a society of people who were taking responsibility for their human state, then we would not live in a society of people with malevolence in their hearts, not to mention the effects that parasitic entities have on us, which often influence us to do the wrong thing.

Nonetheless, such a society will need to discover its own punishments and forms of rehabilitation for murder, rape, stealing, lying, and for other wrongdoing. It could well be that a conscious civilization creates punishments that are not so much barbaric, but so truly raw and psychologically taxing that people would never dare to attempt murder. For example, if you murdered someone, perhaps you would have to talk to all their friends and family about their loss and apologize to each of them. This may be a gauntlet of hundreds of people that you would have to make amends with individually. This process might take years and would be extremely emotionally taxing as you would be exposed to the pain of all these people's loss. Then there is the social stigma of being a murderer that few would want to live with in any conscious society. In many Middle Eastern societies, people would never dream of stealing, as the shame it would bring upon their family is just too great. Presumably, if there were to be incarceration in a new society, it would not just be incarceration but true rehabilitation with a certain level of emotionally and psychologically taxing processes that people have to go through until they are deemed fit to return to society.

City living vs country living

Cities have some clear social and psychological advantages, as the high density of people allows for expanded levels of community and communication. There are unexpected surprises—opportunities to meet new people, experience new things, carry out interesting activities, and eat new food. Country living cannot typically offer as much novelty or quality of human culture—or so it is generally thought. We must consider how to create an element of novelty and excitement within country living.

Some say that living on the land is enough, that hard work, good food, and good people are all human beings need to be happy. But human beings are easily discontented. They become lazy; they start drinking or become addicted to cannabis, and fall into indolence. People in communities can stagnate, become begrudging and disenfranchised, forming alliances and separating from one another.

Has atomized civilization made us all so selfish, petty, and unbearable that, at times, harmonious community living does not even appear possible? Do we need to put a time limit on communities? How do we make communities dynamic and enable the resolution of personal differences? How do we allow people to grow, truly see each other, and be part of something bigger than themselves? How do we allow individuals to carry out work outside the community but also have access to a circle of people to know and be known by? Within the confines of a community, there must be some sharing with the outside world—an interaction, an interface. Without such sharing, the community can easily become insular and stagnant. We need access to many people, and for those people to come into our world. We also need to go outside our community and explore the novelty of different people.

The tribal structure of a community—say 50 to a maximum of 150 people—could work very well[15]. If we bring back working together, there are always projects to be done involving making contact with the elements of the earth. These projects may take one hour, maybe a few hours, maybe all day, but at least you spend time together, truly being with one another. There should also be the development of advanced forms of play, where we can find out what we are each made of and learn about each other and how we perform in activities that challenge and stimulate us. Play extends our range of beingness and artfulness, and the use of technology can only accentuate and amplify what forms of play we can create. There is also the development and evolution of inner human capabilities and powers so that the physical world

---

[15] Dunbar's Number is a theoretical cognitive limit to the number of stable social relationships an individual can maintain, typically around 150. This concept, proposed by British anthropologist Robin Dunbar, suggests that there is a maximum number of people with whom one can maintain meaningful connections, influenced by the size of the human brain, particularly the neocortex. It implies that as group sizes exceed this number, social cohesion and effective communication diminish.

would then become molded by our thoughts—a kind of dreamscape not unlike virtual reality, but actually a reality in a way few people in our time can comprehend.

The golden age is our potential realized

The Golden Age is not a cliché but the result of harmonious interpersonal alchemy, the collective golden glow of true psychological health. The present age, by and large, is one of sickness: anxiety, neurosis, derision, denial, poverty, abuse, and inequity. It doesn't take much to see that the present human world is out of balance, and the way we live is grossly suboptimal. Yet many people are in denial because our world is the only one they know. They cannot conceive of a truly healthy world, as that would be too confronting to their egos, which would have to realize their own standards were subpar.

The vast majority of people in our world fit into a suboptimal world, are in service to a suboptimal world, and perhaps would not fit into a healthy world. Likewise, many of the most balanced, kind, and sensitive souls do not fit into this current world. We live in a transitory paradox of evolution. In a sense, we are only imperfect monkeys—not imperfect gods, or even indistinct refractions of God. Perhaps it is necessary that we become neither perfect nor imperfect, but creative expressions of the divine potential within us.

A healthy society would not look like a cookie culture of clichéd high achievers, with standardized square jaws and perfect, shiny platinum hair, conformist and conservative in nature. A society of true individuals would mean a flourishing of human warmth, variety, and artistry, but also a peaceful balance and alignment with the cosmos and a natural expression of individuality. In our world of relatively limited tribal affiliations, true individuals are commonly stamped out by ignorant groupthink. In a new world, we would naturally accept and allow the uniqueness of each individual's light and inner nature.

Humans are completed by a community that knows them and wants the best for them. Human beings are in their most essential mode of expression when they can express unconditional love for their fellow human beings. When there is the literal, metaphysical emanation of unconditional love, there is a spiritually functional society in which individuals are energetically activated to radiate their own selfhood into the field of earth and humanity. The only truly sustainable way humanity can live is as one big tribe on Earth, in recognition of the essential unity within the human species and in all life.

Yet for individuals, interpersonal challenges always remain—issues of esteem, communicating one's thoughts and feelings in a compassionate way, saying NO, and navigating the complexities of interpersonal desire, jealousy, and true friendship. Not to mention important questions such as whom you invite to your party and all the difficulties, decisions, and creativity involved in being an actively social human being. We could presume that in such an optimal society, issues such as pedophilia, war, and drug addiction would largely be relics of the past.

Humanity has historically appeared addicted to war, and war, at times, may have been an antidote to an often boring existence. With the development of AI and advanced drones, humanity has largely taken the skill, strategy, and art out of warfare, so warfare only becomes merely a matter of which side has the better programmers and engineers. Sophisticated war games or sports are surely good enough to replace an arena for developing one's skill and strategy, but would a civilized society allow such games to be "do or die"? Even so, some people seem addicted to risking their lives, and extreme sports show us how important the high adrenaline of "do or die" is to many. Death would continue to be heartbreaking, and physical health issues would still present themselves—but probably much less so if we were to become conscious of what it means to be truly healthy.

The human drama must be made more conscious and held in context and understanding, rather than engaged within a victimized, self-destructive, and narrowing unconsciousness. Developing oneself as an artist is a challenge, and being oneself is the greatest challenge—and often the two are interchangeable. There are also vocational challenges, learning challenges, and challenges in choosing to live with one another. These are challenges that very few people in our present society are up to facing. Many people find the life of getting along with others and their communities just too hard. Humans are complex emotional beings, and so we need to plumb these depths. People need to express themselves, live with purpose, and be recognized and respected for who they truly are. Do we now even know what optimal human functioning is, or how that would appear? Nobody can say we do, but many of us can say we have glimpsed higher human functioning after ingesting psychedelics.

The bad guys and sharks

As it is, we live in a society where the bad guys and sharks appear to be a somewhat necessary part of the collective scenario. Such critters are a stimulus that brings us off our hammocks, eating bananas. Nobody with any sense wants to live in a world where we are solely lying in hammocks and eating bananas, yet we live in a world where many people are grossly overworked and desire to pursue that illusion. We must choose to get off the hammock and be actively engaged and enriched in meaningful endeavours so that we don't need the sharks and bad guys to shock us out of our complacency.

Intimacy, relationships, and true community are perhaps the most challenging arenas for human beings—much more challenging than facing down the bad guys—because we must be vulnerable and put our hearts on the line when coming into a relationship and community. With bad guys, we can remain hardened, and less is at stake. We must choose the challenge of community, though, and clearly those closest to us will challenge us much more than the bad guys, who are so much further from the realities of our hearts.

Sometimes people are difficult, but what if they were truly committed to working through the issues that present themselves? There would be many interpersonal challenges in a sustainable society, and the challenges would transform and expand in different ways—something that should be welcomed. We need to keep in mind that this system must be based on the premise that individual and collective growth are the most necessary human foundations. Our present "free-range" society of unaccountability, without true communication and intimacy between group members, means that people can get away with a lot of inconsistency and behavior they know is far from optimal, to say the least. What we need is a new culture of mutual respect and sensitivity to human awareness—and to its truest and most essential spiritual and human needs.

If individuals in the new world decide to start acting in ways that are unhealthy—for example, by abusing others, continually treating others disrespectfully, engaging in psychopathic behavior, and disturbing the peace in the most unconscious way—it is up to the community to support that person into a healthy way of being. Our present society does not truly support people who need help, as we do not relate to each other as being part of a singular humanity.

For people to be truly lovable, we must create the conditions for them to be self-reflective, aware, and empowered to make necessary changes autonomously. In other words, people must have the drive and initiative to work on their own character. We need to enable a society in which we live with people who can truly be trusted. Our environment must foster and encourage communicative abilities and facilitate the growth of people who are useful to themselves, to each other, and to the world.

CHAPTER 8: SYSTEMS FOR LIFE

The Nature of Paradise

Human beings have always had an idea of some sort of paradise where there are no problems, but that is not the way life works. In certain phases of human growth, problems may become starker. You see your own way of operating more clearly, and interpersonal issues become more perplexing and intricate. Essentially, we are called to communicate and express the essence of who we are, but to do so authentically rather than selfishly. We are called to make difficult decisions in how to act and what to say, and to learn how to navigate and negotiate tricky situations where it may not be straightforward to know what to say and do.

If we are to be respectful as human beings, we have to be sensitive and consider various emotional, mental, and psychological tensions in the people around us. We are simultaneously called to self-actualization and to think less about ourselves and more about other people in our society: to have others' best interests in mind by acting with a spirit of sharing, caring, and goodwill. These are qualities that humanity has always held in the highest regard, and when expressed, ultimately lead to the manifestation of the individual's best interests, which means that unselfishness is ultimately selfishness. In a collective sense, sharing, caring, and goodwill lead to the most desirable outcomes for the human species, rather than our strained, illogical, adversarial, and mean spirited survival based programs.

Transformation as a Rule

In a genuinely free society, there would not be any control of people's use of currency, as some may recognize multiple currencies as containers of value and energy. However, perhaps we should ensure that energy and value move within our society, as hoarding and accumulation could be perceived as a kind of mental illness. Perhaps, rather than increasing in value over time, currency should decrease in value over time until that energy—or currency—has no value, which should inspire people to spend it[16]. In that case, currency evaporates over time or rots like fruit, and perhaps the value of the currency decreases ten percent every month. A system such as this ensures we focus on the present, rather than relying on creating "security" in the form of money. In a sane global society, everyone is already secure, and we are all living in a way that would not rely on money to provide security. Clearly, every form of monetary accumulation, stock market trading, currency trading—or simply put, making money from money—then becomes invalid and fruitless, as there is literally no fruit that comes from it. Again, we must live in a society where the amount of currency and the value of things are determined first by the presence of the people and resources on Earth.

In a healthy society, everyone has what they need to learn and to live. Just like any well-functioning big tribe of human beings who live without money, the global human tribe must live the same way, where money is not the focus of our survival; only our collective actions are. We must remember that in the tribe there is always security, and people largely have what they need to survive and thrive in that society.

---

[16] This idea is discussed in a book called *What comes after money?* (2011) edited by Daniel Pinchbeck and Ken Jordan.

People must also work on behalf of the tribe to enable that security. In such a tribal situation, you are expected to pull your weight, and the more value you bring to the group, the more the tribe values you. In a sane society, people would be able to optimize their own lifestyles to facilitate the most growth and happiness for themselves, and they wouldn't need money to do that. In a sane society, people would focus on what truly has value in their lives and cultivate those values. However, it makes sense that the next iteration of our civilization is to create a system or multiple systems, whereby we rule over money and not let it rule over us collectively. When we have all learned the lessons of money and truly transcended the need for it, then we could let it go—presumably in 50 to 100 years.

The politics of Interconnection

Whenever different people come together in a group, there can often be friction because there are many different types of thoughts, emotions, and views. Religion and other forms of ideology often attempt to stamp out such differences to create an artificial kind of unity, which does not typically allow the growth of the individual in their distinctiveness and difference. We need to consider how to live with one another as a community, as a humanity, as a global human culture—simply as human beings—but not using the glue of shared belief systems. This is certainly a challenging enterprise, as anyone who has been involved in any kind of conscious community can attest. Even though living tribally is our baseline state of existence, it is a tricky thing for us to do—to track and take care of multitudes of different relationships and tend to them all, without letting enmity and complex emotional reactions and actions muddy and distort our network of relationships.

Many people in the modern world seek a partner to complete them. Perhaps what truly completes an individual is not just one person but a whole tribe or greater family of people. In a truly humanly connected society, you could choose to be part of a tribal group, which you are voluntarily tied to for a certain amount of time—perhaps even for a lifetime. We should also understand that learning not only comes from those of one's kin but from the intermingling of kin and types. We need to think about living not just tribally but also in cities, environments where we may not know everyone. Many human beings appear to have a need for the novelty of "the unknown" in other people, rather than just being surrounded by familiar people.

It would make sense to create a database of society that could be so intelligent in terms of how each of us is internally mapped, that upon reaching a certain age—say 21—you could be partnered with someone perfectly suited to you, or perhaps given access to environments where you could meet a person right for you. In our current society, partnerships are either arranged or we randomly find a partner we like. We make love and have children, but this is clearly not an intelligent way—to just leave it up to the individual or their parents to hunt for a partner.

In a post-capitalist, post-consumer world, we need to ask, "What are the optimal conditions for individuals?" We should consider that monogamy may not be ideal for everyone, and that, in a truly free society, some individuals would seek other sexual partners as part of their growth and learning about themselves—as is already the case. There is a sexual revolution within us that prioritizes intimacy beyond physicality. We should consider how this expression of love will change as society evolves. First of all, teenagers must be able to explore the potential of interpersonal intimacy, and we must give females and males effective natural contraception that do not interfere with their hormones. We must facilitate dialogue and communication between human beings, which will enable us to collectively hit the right notes and strike the right chords in our community.

"How do we love each other?" is one of the most primary questions we need to be asking. Much of the answer is to enable society to create lovable people so we can enable the flourishing of the soul in individuals. Then people can truly understand themselves, be honest, and not cause suffering for others, allowing others to realize themselves as well. We must tear down the barriers between us to eliminate tension between people so a deeper, more spiritual apprehension of the meaning of the relationship can occur. Then we can truly understand how we are in a relationship with other people. Within that intelligence, in that recognized collective understanding, is where freedom lies. Humanity is now largely enslaved in ignorance—not truly living the meaning of love and the meaning of human relationships and their potential, which are necessary for the flourishing of the soul. Transcendence through connection and communion within a field we can now barely conceive of would be one of great collective sensitivity—and a space that some of us may have touched through participating in events and places in our present world.

The raising of children

We also need to seriously consider the raising of children. In a sane society where people live close to one another, children may be raised as much by the community as by two parents. Children should truly be recognized as assets in a community—not just of their parents but of the whole community—with the understanding that people want to invest in these assets with time and care. Perhaps children could be integrated into all of society and mentored by many members of society, not just designated teachers. Leaving the raising of children to only two people, who may not be particularly suitable for the task, might not be the best option. So much stress is put upon "the family" from the conservative viewpoint, but we must ask: What is the basis of the values that create the family? Perhaps community or tribe is more fundamental than family.

How is the community to raise children? How can children learn from different adults? People who like to look after children may be older people, parents who are about to have children, or even older children. We need to identify what each child needs and then deliver it to them. We should celebrate motherhood and allow mothers to give full attention to their children rather than simply "working," if that is not in their interest. We also need to free mothers from their motherhood duties at times, so they can live, be, and relate with other people, not just their children. We also need to truly acknowledge the role of fatherhood, but mostly, the importance of attentively raising and educating children far beyond the scope of our present models of education.

We should first teach children to communicate. What is reading and writing, after all, but communication? We then also need to build scenarios of what communication is for, especially regarding how to be a human being in relationships. Some schools may come close to facilitating this type of learning, but it is clear that such learning should be universally cultivated. Children first need to learn to be human beings, not just workers or overseers of workers, as capitalism typically demands. Children especially need to learn in a hands—on manner, not just abstractly. They need to build things, grow food, and play. Whatever is fun is best.

Science needs to be practical for them. They would do well to learn life skills that are useful—massage, cooking, gardening, building houses, living skills, and surviving in the wild. They need to learn cooperation, meditation, stillness, and activity. Learning to communicate with plants and animals is essential. Music, drama, and art must be primary (rather than secondary) to foster each person's understanding of their potential as creators.

Without forcefulness and a bottom line of strict adherence to presumed practicality, the children's own will can come to the fore. Without indoctrination and rote learning, individual intelligence flourishes. Let the children speak, and let us listen to them. Also, let us speak to them and allow them to interact with the community fluidly, catalyzing curiosity as the most significant aspect of learning. Then they will continue to learn for their entire lives. Learning should occur through fun and fellowship. The choice and desire to direct oneself with others allows self-discovery. If society itself weren't such a grindstone, then we would have no need to bring children back to that grindstone, so then we can inspire children to find their own will. In a post-grindstone world, it is this will and desire to act that creates the wondrousness we need in our lives, as much as we need oxygen. We should give children parameters and the ability to contribute to the adult world. We should teach children how to think, and also how to retain information in the most practical sense—for example, how to measure and carry out real experiments as a scientist does. Discipline and focus come naturally when you are doing things you want to do, not forced into things you do not want to do.

Forums in a true democracy

Many people don't want a government or to be governed. The government is, at times, like a mafia, and taxes are synonymous with protection money, with most of that tax money going to the war machine in many countries. In most countries, you get little back from the money your government takes from you. However, it would appear that we do need leaders in human society, and we do need to decide all manner of things collectively. Yet leaders will emerge naturally within a sane society. That emergence will happen socially, once individuals are able to perceive and understand who is most capable of empowering others, and who best possesses a creative and ethical sense of direction. Within society, there seems to be a need for different forums to decide and do things, such as in a true democracy, when the decisions are taken by the people on "what needs to be done." If there were many different real-world and online spaces of true discussion, then people could be truly involved in how society is created, and true leaders would naturally emerge in the thoughtful intercourse.

How to breed people

We need to see the affinities between different people. This is a primary challenge of a global culture so that people do not just remain within their own culture or genetic racial group. Intermingling and intermarrying are the recipe for peace and goodwill between races—and perhaps also for genetic strength, not just homogeneity. However, the majority of people may want to associate with people from their own race or culture, and this is only natural, one would think.

Certainly, with dog or horse breeding, you do not mix your breeds willy-nilly but combine certain breeds with certain qualities. Rather than just "muttifying" our global human population into a homogeneous blend, we need to think about the various qualities and characteristics of each race—its strengths and weaknesses—something we humans can do with dogs, but appear to have difficulty doing for ourselves. Perhaps the issue is that our value systems have not evolved enough to understand what truly has value in a human, so nuanced conversations about race can become offensive to some. If we could understand, in a global civilization, what we valued in a race, perhaps we would think about how to preserve such races or breed them with other races to effectively make whole new breeds of humans.

Living euthanasia

We know that people without challenges can become complacent. At this stage in our evolution, we cannot just go back to a time when hardship and trauma shaped people's character. We must also remember that hardship, abuse, and a difficult life just as often shape people into sociopaths and generally dysfunctional people, as they can create people of character. Yet people are perhaps most functional when they are up against something that tests their strengths and weaknesses. Therefore, we must explore how to create challenges, trials, and initiations within human life that sterile modern life largely lacks. It appears there needs to be a liveliness, a quickening heartbeat, an edge—a danger that might involve suffering. Humans want to face challenges: artistic challenges, group challenges, challenges in learning, working together, emotional challenges, and challenges in sports and games. There is also something in us that seeks a sense of adventure and requires a wild space—an untamed area with large elements beyond our control, or even beyond our understanding. Is this edge in outer space, just like in Star Trek, or can we manufacture it and integrate this understanding into ourselves and our own relationships with each other?

Warfare and disease have traditionally taken out the weak and foolish within human societies. One of the issues with modern-day society is that it has had fewer events to weed out so-called undesirable elements. Now we live in a society where the weeds appear to proliferate. Perhaps we could create a sense of imperative whereby people are motivated not to fall behind. If society were to euthanize 0.2 percent of the weakest and least capable of the population every year, then such a society would continue to get stronger. Over 100 years, this would account for 20 percent of the potential population. This euthanizing would require testing, which could perhaps apply only to people who are between 15 and 25 years of age, in the prime of their lives, and they could be tested yearly. If you were 25, you would then see that maybe two percent of your contemporaries did not make it. This would not be so much of a toll upon society, especially if it were within a framework of "do or die," within a truly fair test and initiation that people agreed to participate in. This would give such a society a true edge—a seriousness that would eradicate any kind of indolence and motivate people to bring their best to the table and to truly raise the bar.

If we lived in a sane society, we would all know that death was not the end—and because people would not fear death, all people would be invested in a non-fearful perspective about death. We need to think in terms of the whole, and yet also zero in on the concerns of the individual. If you were going to be operated on by a brain surgeon, would you want the surgeon who was in the bottom two percent of their class? Even a surgeon from the bottom ten percent would be a concern. If you were a person who was in the bottom two percent of your society in terms of aptitude, capability, and likeability, you would also very likely be among the unhappier people within that society.

Even though this may sound inhumane, we need to think of the wider health of the overall populace and consider this sacrifice. It could also be something of an antidote to a sterile civilisation living in cotton wool, insulated from death. If we didn't choose to do this, then there would be an increasing divide between those "at the top" and those "at the bottom," and how else could we maintain the genetic fitness of our civilization? We can do everything we can to promote fitness, but continual pruning of those of us who are the least performing members of society is going to ensure that we are guiding reproduction wisely and improving the fitness of the human species. The Georgia Guidestones[17] very rightly communicate this as an imperative in a new civilization.

---

[17] Though a lot of people baulk at the general nature of the Georgia Guidestones tenets, "unite humanity with a living new language" demonstrates a great deal of spiritual insight and many people can resonate with the visionary nature of what they communicate.
- Maintain humanity under 500,000,000 in perpetual balance with nature.
- Guide reproduction wisely—improving fitness and diversity.
- Unite humanity with a living new language.
- Rule passion, faith, tradition, and all things with tempered reason.
- Protect people and nations with fair laws and just courts.
- Let all nations rule internally resolving external disputes in a world court.
- Avoid petty laws and useless officials.
- Balance personal rights with social duties.
- Prize truth, beauty, love—seeking harmony with the infinite.
- Be not a cancer on the Earth. Leave room for nature.

Interestingly, these guidelines present the idea that humanity WILL be brought to a population under 500 million as a fait accompli—a given. Thus, the stones are apparently written from a prophetic standpoint. Some interpret the stones as being put there by the cabal or Illuminati, yet nobody really knows who wrote the guidelines.

CHAPTER 9: HOW TO LIVE

Hard work and play

We are enslaved by the idea of "hard work" and by the necessity of "self-sacrifice" within work. In many cultures, work has become a kind of evil addiction. Work becomes glorified, but what are we glorifying? Many people are avoiding personal growth with overwork. When human beings are not working, they may need to look hard at themselves, and very few appear to know how to do this. If we are to live in a culture of sane and conscious people, we must examine ourselves—self-reflecting and taking action in our inner and outer lives regarding what we see.

As a species, we should define our purpose and set up an agreed—upon list of things we need to do. Unhindered by commercial imperatives, we could build beautiful buildings and spaces in the physical world. Cities today are not created as art. With few exceptions, buildings are designed as "economically" as possible. In order to create things like fans, cars, and computers, automated processes and robots can take over, so that humans don't have to do mindless and repetitive work—unless they want to and find value in that. We should take the time and find the resources to eradicate such drone-like work. Then nobody would have to do it, and this would be recognized as a collective reward if we truly recognize our interconnectedness.

We should give artists and visionaries the power to imagine new possibilities so that we can create novelty and beauty, inspiring people and helping them reach their potential. We can go to the galaxies and advance our species to connect with other races in the universe.

We need to recognize where individuals truly are in their lives and honor them with positions that serve their highest good. If everyone has more or less the same capabilities or abilities in a society, that would be boring and simply unrealistic. It is imperative to have elders, to have those who are of high achievement. In any given field, for example, carpentry or martial arts, there are those who have achieved a very high level of skill. This normally accords with age. There are always going to be some artisans and artists whose work is much more highly esteemed than that of other artists, or sportspeople who are a cut above the others. This is a natural state of affairs.

Co-operating with nature's world

Cooperation with nature needs to be a primary aspect of creating a sustainable human future. If technology were the area of our primary future excitement… wouldn't that be boring? It is in the interface and relationship with nature and the real world that we connect more with our sense of innate becoming and happiness. Is real happiness boring? Happiness should be the least boring and most fulfilling thing. Real happiness could be perceived as the aliveness of a human being full of information and able to communicate that living information.

What is boring anyway? Boredom could be perceived as a person lacking fulfillment, lacking contentment, and a sense of place and purpose. Or we could perceive that boredom is caused by being shielded, closed down, and numb in preparation for psychic attack.

In a relatively frictionless, ideal world, what would be the elements that drive people to do better—to be better? There clearly is an innate drive within us, and you can see it in the best of us. Chances are, those who have this drive are doing better and being better in their lives and are authentically growing. We must amplify what is important and what allows each of us to grow, rather than just having to deal with transactional, mistrustful, mechanical behavior. We must also honor the basis of our survival drives—sex, money, and power—and allow people to be rewarded and come to a balance of these forces within themselves.

In the new world, we need to allow people to engage in an enchanted state of being—outside the realm of survival—so they may flower spiritually. Our present culture keeps us bound to problem-solving states, which can be useful, but they are clearly limited states. We would do well to recognize that some people are working in realms of expanded consciousness. Our present society lobotomizes these people with pharmaceuticals and labels them as abnormal. We need to let our shamans flower to their full potential by creating safe spaces for them to grow and expand. Such people are the super-athletes of the spiritual world, and if we do not support them and allow them to grow, all of us suffer, and we do not know the potential of our spiritual and psychic growth.

Greed and egotism need not be present in the global human tribe. In fact, we should create systems that naturally discourage and shun these qualities, just as these tendencies are shunned in any tribal society. True self-interest is the development of oneself and the sharing of one's values—not the accumulation of cars and big houses. What is required of people in a global tribe is that they take responsibility for their own evolution, rather than needing a threat to confront or challenge them to gather momentum. We need to challenge each other consciously—to grow and not be complacent. If time is our most precious commodity, then self-interest is a life well-lived, not necessarily being a captain of industry chained to great responsibility and having no time to live.

Self-governing initiations

Many people need an external program that encourages their growth, whether that be schooling, a workshop, or going into business. Many do not have the self-discipline to challenge themselves. There is something compelling in passing through a system of learning that is, in a sense, predetermined. This is how many clubs and organizations operate, where you receive markers along the way in order to signify your learning. A good example is the Boy Scouts—their badges are degrees of recognized status. Most traditional cultures have such status symbols: tiers and phases of undertaking which recognize a person's capabilities, aligning with being allowed to participate in certain events or access certain parts of the landscape.

Our society already has such tiers, such as levels of schooling. But these "badges" are limited. What if there were a wide range of tiers and achievement levels that enabled you to be recognized as capable in different fields or frameworks? Perhaps there could be layers or levels of personal achievement, or recognition of internal qualities or human capabilities.

How do we maintain the standard that we could attain in a civilization where people are self-actualized and largely self-governed, while living in harmony with the natural world? How would we prevent corruption and weakness in such a society? The checks and balances that global society gives itself should be in the form of adequate feedback, appropriate testing, and scientific scrutiny. We must all have the facility for providing feedback and criticism in a manner that is not condemning, but allows improvement and self—reflection concerning our relevant actions and creations. Within a framework outside of the tyranny and control typical of our world, a "gamification" of society's system—similar to a "social credit" system—cannot easily be denied as being sensible in any intelligent society. The gamification of many systems within society must inspire people to live better and work better, rather than control or hinder, or punish them in unreasonable ways. A sane society would inspire and reward people with incentives, instead of punishing them for not meeting standards, making mistakes, or not following the established protocols.

What if, in our new global society, large sectors of society begin to adopt ideology or religion? Or if some sectors of society go down a purely dark and destructive path, what would the rules or laws be, and how would they be enforced? How would we acknowledge free will and exploration, and yet also individually and collectively say, "enough is enough," and put a foot down to stop activities and endeavors that are clearly harmful to the collective consciousness? The point is, it is up to everyone to govern themselves, and for the collective to govern itself. There can be an understanding that some ways are better than others. Some ways are also harmful—which can be demonstrated. At times, collective errors might have to be made by the majority to see what is not the way. The only way to remedy all of this is to have proper communication feedback mechanisms in place, where the voice of the people and the voices of sanity and reason are encouraged.

Agreeing to disagree

In a functional society where each human being is respected and included, there shouldn't be too many major issues. Still, bad things can happen—really big mistakes in which people die, and major conflicts and disagreements are a part of human life. Often, we need to be able to agree to disagree and find a solution that might involve compromise. Conflicts that arise between individuals and groups in society shouldn't be conducted in mechanical courtrooms but in human mediation and investigation that requires accountability and change. It is not that there should be some "state" or ideology interfering in people's affairs. However, when push comes to shove and one or both parties request it, rather than having to go to civil courts, for example, over marriage breakups requiring lawyers, there could be more mediation, reflection, and advice given from different wise parties. If we lived in a society where people desired to grow, rather than just being right or remaining fixed in their perspectives, differences between people and groups could be mediated and guided in a more humane and personal way— in a way that recognizes all the multifaceted aspects of our being and all our truest needs.

Working with other people in relationships—within the vagaries and complexities where our inner world meets the inner world of others—helps us address the specific and the personal. Working with the blade of the plow or the sword is so much simpler than facing the internal world. This is, of course, the masculine agenda. It has been a man's world. A pure patriarchy doesn't work, but neither is a matriarchy the answer. It is only in the masculine and feminine working together whereby balance is obtained in the natural order of being. When masculine and feminine principles are clearly defined, humanity will come into a much clearer cosmic resolution.

Cultural change

In a sustainable global culture, where the internal values and reasons of human beings are king, traditional cultures would be recognised, valued, and learned from. We also need to recognize the value of creativity, new culture, and new ways of being in any given place. Too often, historical cultures represent the only way and are inhibitive of growth or change. The global consumer culture of the marketplace, which makes everywhere on Earth a homogeneous mall parking lot, does not lead us anywhere satisfying. Change is a constant. Though we can take refuge in what doesn't change and has not changed for centuries, there are always challenges that require flexibility in approach and intent. For example, if Japan's current population of 130 million were reduced by 99% (to 125,000), people in Japan could much more effectively manage their cultural life. What would remain of the old culture? What would they keep? What new cultures and practices would the Japanese people create in that land?

The end of religion

Religion is problematic because, when we have differing belief systems, people act and think differently. They worship in different temples, inherently causing separation, conflict, and division. Yet diversity is not the problem. The issues begin when people separate from one another in the practice of different beliefs that are rigidly set and do not allow any flexibility or freedom of thought. The way religion is practiced by many today could be perceived as a kind of mental illness, because these fixed beliefs prevent people from thinking and therefore learning for themselves—and essentially being themselves. In an evolved society filled with people who think for themselves, you would hope that people would not resort to dogma and fixed beliefs, but instead endeavor to be flexible and free-minded.

The truth is not in rigid belief systems, nor in the religion itself, which originally was just fingers pointing at the moon. Within religion, the enforced structures and rules that aim to control and limit human expression are clearly a real issue. Jiddu Krishnamurti's famous words, "Truth is a pathless land," communicate a great deal. No doubt, religious teachings were valuable and useful in the times they were first communicated. Could we envision a new world where old teachings coexist with people living directly from their own intelligence? It would appear that the words of people living now are more useful for us than words recorded hundreds or even thousands of years ago.

The map is not the territory; the finger pointing at the moon is not the moon. It is not hard to appreciate the grandiosity and rich tapestry of the world's religions, but it does not appear that we can take them with us into the new world. What use would we have for them? Why would they be necessary? If we have truly absorbed and understood the wisdom within these teachings, why would we need to hang on to them or keep referring to the texts as if there were more to learn? Shouldn't we create opportunities for learning within life itself? Shouldn't all of human life be a kind of religious ritual?

It does appear that intelligent people live most effectively without religion most effectively, having shed the ideologies of religious dogma, while learning to trust their own intelligence and intuition. Taking life as it comes and maintaining one's own spiritual connection and internal ethic doesn't require some reference to rules and ideas from a dusty book. Religions typically teach that there is another reality, a spiritual reality much bigger than the earthly reality, and these religions provide moral precepts that can help societies to effectively function. However, religions can also work to prevent and inhibit human beings from exploring and understanding what it is to be human. Moral codes can become prisons. Ontological insecurity, which is not structured, is our natural state. None of our thoughts or ideas can ever be the truth—if such a thing truly exists. Our thoughts and ideas can only represent truth. As such, we would do well to explore truth in the way an artist does.

Being human through it all

What we call "human nature" is typically only the acts of the misguided, foolish, or unintelligent. There is no error in the inherent nature of human beings, who are essentially good and true, because all else is folly and not as enjoyable. What is often called human nature represents the vagaries and potential wanderings of the beast—with its follies and errors—not its most essential or true nature of what a human can be. If we are to create a sane culture, we must create a culture that discourages greed, ego, and power rather than encouraging these tendencies. We must encourage the benefits and value of cooperation and fellowship rather than conflict, and we must encourage a correct use of our life and inspiration to utilize the powers of relating, intimacy, friendship, and sexuality.

At the end of each day, we would find ourselves the same as we were before. We are human beings; we have bodies that need food, clothing, and shelter. But we would no longer be obligated to work for so many hours. Because we have a social and practical foundation for life, we are able to fulfill our higher needs—social, cultural, artistic, spiritual, psychic, and intergalactic.

We would then all have a chance to be happy—to fulfill our most essential needs: to love, grow, and be met by our own kind. We can also work together as a species and experience true belonging, in the understanding that we are at home in life on Earth, and we can make Earth as we choose it to be. In fact, we must LIVE—in a Golden Age[18]. Humanity is indeed doomed to perfection.

---

[18] The Golden Age is a concept talked about in many ancient civilizations and represents a universal human longing for a time of ideal conditions where people live in peace, there is an abundance of resources and human beings live in moral integrity. Some civilizations have experienced temporary Golden Ages, however, what is at hand is the possibility to create a truly sustainable Global Golden Age.

www.ingramcontent.com/pod-product-compliance
Lightning Source LLC
Chambersburg PA
CBHW060500080526
44584CB00015B/1496